THE MAKING OF A PROPHET, PRIEST, AND KING

A Study Guide on First Samuel

DIANE RAFFERTY

ISBN 978-1-68570-972-3 (paperback)
ISBN 978-1-68570-973-0 (digital)

Christian Faith Publishing
832 Park Avenue
Meadville, PA 16335
www.christianfaithpublishing.com

Printed in the United States of America

As newborn babes, long for spiritual milk, so that by it
you may grow toward salvation—now that you have
tasted that the Lord is good. As you come to Him, a living
stone rejected by men but chosen by God and precious, you also,
as living stones, are being built up as a spiritual house—a
holy priesthood to offer up spiritual sacrifices
acceptable to God through Messiah Yeshua (Jesus Christ).

—1 Peter 2:2–5 TLV (notation mine)

Contents

Recommended Study Aids

- Bible
- Maps of Old Testament Israel and the surrounding nations (back of your Bible is fine)

Welcome to an In-depth Study of First Samuel

The lives of Samuel, Saul, and David are interwoven in the book of First Samuel. Each of these men's lives was changed after they had a personal encounter with God and then with each other. Some of the changes were beneficial to them and the nation of Israel, but other changes brought negative results within their families as well as the people living within Israel's territories.

The wonderful thing about the Bible is that God made sure the reader is told the whole story: the good and the bad. These men were real people, and the book of First Samuel reveals their strengths and their weaknesses.

As you read the passages, remember to put yourself into the story/event to better understand the person's choices, attitudes, and actions. Claim any promises for yourself, obey any direction that the Holy Spirit leads you to take, and be encouraged by the examples of these men and women who did great and mighty things in the anointing power of the Lord. I encourage you to do all of the *bonus study* sections offered in each chapter to go even further into the background of a topic. The more Scriptures you look up, the deeper your understanding will become.

It is also very important to pray *every time* before you study the word of God and ask the Holy Spirit to open your mind to help you understand what He wants you to learn and how to can apply it in your life. Second Peter 1:20–21 assures us that the Holy Spirit wrote all of Scripture through many different men, but God's message remains the same: He loves you and wants you to know Him in a personal relationship.

WELCOME TO AN IN-DEPTH STUDY OF FIRST SAMUEL

In 2 Timothy 3:16–17, Paul tells Timothy that *all* scripture is to be used to teach, train, and equip the believer so this guide will use both the Old and New Testaments to study the book of First Samuel. I hope you enjoy the study.

Blessings,
Diane

Background of the Book
of First Samuel

In the Hebrew Bible, First and Second Samuel is one book. In the second-century BC, the *Septuagint* (group of seventy men) translated the book from the original Hebrew text into Greek and split it into two books at that time.[1] This study deals with the first book division, which was written around 930 BC, and covers a time span of approximately one hundred forty years. It was written by several authors, but no one knows for sure who wrote which part. It is assumed that Samuel wrote the events up to the time of his own death (1 Samuel 25). We know that Samuel wrote at least one book as noted in 1 Samuel 10:25, and in 1 Chronicles 29:29, we are told the other possible authors are the prophets Gad and Nathan.

From the time when Joshua brought the Israelites into the Promised Land, and the twelve tribes of Israel settled into their own apportioned plots, every man did what was right in his own eyes (see Judges 21:25). When the Israelites got into trouble, God would provide a judge to deliver them from their enemies, and then they would follow that person's leadership for many years. Some of the judges that led Israel for forty years were Othniel (Caleb's nephew), Ehud, Shamgar, Deborah, and Gideon. Samson judged Israel for twenty years, and there were others who served in this role for only a few years. The book of Judges covers the three hundred fifty years from Joshua to Eli and Samuel who were the last men to hold the official title of Judge in Israel.

We are told in 1 Samuel 4:18 that Eli judged Israel for forty years. According to the Bible (postflood), a generation could range from one hundred years (Genesis 15:13–16) to thirty-eight years

(Deuteronomy 2:14). Therefore, during the forty years, each judge was the person God used to speak to their own generation. Read Acts 13:36 to see that David was considered to be the man for his generation.

Am I Someone that God Can Use to Speak to My Generation Today?

The book of First Samuel is really one storyline about three men: Samuel, whose entire life was given to God's service; Saul, who is insecure, proud, and rebellious at heart; and David, who is a brave, creative warrior with a heart to honor God. The book of First Samuel weaves these three lives together into a dramatic and entertaining tale of love and loss as well as victory and defeat. It is easy when reading this book to feel like you are in the middle of a movie or weekly television drama. There is a *lot* of drama and high emotion within this book. Here are just a few of the topics that you will read about:

- Sister wives (polygamy)
- Barrenness (infertility)
- Mental health issues
- Political intrigues
- Friendship/loyalty
- Sinful spiritual leaders
- Dysfunctional family dynamics

There are *four main characters* in First Samuel: Eli, Samuel, Saul, and David. There are also *four supporting characters*: Hannah, Hophni, Phinehas (Eli's sons), and Jonathan. Here is a short bio for each character.

Eli

He is a Levitical priest who judged Israel for forty years in the town of Shiloh where the tent of meeting (created under Moses's supervision in the wilderness) and the Ark of the Covenant were set up. (See Exodus 25–27.) We are told in 1 Samuel 2:22 that Eli was very old at the time Hannah met him, and in 1 Samuel 3:2, it tells us that Eli's eyesight was growing dim and he could no longer see well. By chapter 4:15, Eli is ninety-eight years old and fully blind. In 1 Samuel 4:18, we learn that he weighed so much that when he fell backward off his chair, he broke his neck in the fall. Eli didn't like the evil things his sons were doing, but he honored them above God and that was his downfall. (See 1 Samuel 2:23–25, 29–30.)

Samuel

His name means *God heard or name of God.*[2] He was a *miracle baby*, prayed for by his mother, Hannah, and given by God for a special purpose. Samuel served as a helper (eyes and ears) to Eli the priest from approximately age three until Eli's death. When Samuel turned thirty (ordained age to serve), he became a priest and the judge of Israel (1 Samuel 3:19–21). Samuel lived a *normal life*; he had his own home, was married, and had children. He served God from early childhood until his death from old age. (See 1 Samuel 7:15, 25:1.) He was from the Levitical tribe of Kohath (Numbers 4:1–4, 1 Chronicles 6:33–38) and had two sons who were also priests, but Joel and Abijah did not serve the Lord well (just like Eli's sons, 1 Samuel 8:1–3). Samuel made his home in Ramah, perhaps on the same property of his parents and relatives.

Saul

He was from the tribe of Benjamin and possibly left-handed (Judges 20:14–16; 1 Chronicles 12:1–2). He worked for his father and had a wife named Ahinoam who bore him four boys and two girls (1 Samuel 14:49, 31:2; 2 Samuel 2:8). Saul also had at least one concubine (Rizpah) who bore him at least two sons (2 Samuel 3:7, 21:8). In 1 Samuel 13:1 (NASB), it says that Saul was forty years old when he became king and reigned thirty-two years. In 1 Samuel 13:1 (KJV), it states that Saul reigned one year; and then in his second year, he gathered men (including his oldest son Jonathan) for an army to fight against the Philistines. Saul had many emotional/mental problems that plagued him throughout his life.

David

He was the youngest son of eight boys born to Jesse in Bethlehem. David was the great-grandson of Boaz and Ruth. David spent most of his youth as a shepherd, watching over his father's flocks. He was a gifted musician who wrote many songs and poems that can be found in the Old Testament book of Psalms. At the time of meeting Goliath, David was an older teenager (nineteen?). Saul moved David into his household after defeating Goliath, and after some time, he began to go out to war (had to be twenty or older to be in the army) and married Saul's youngest daughter, Michal, soon afterward. David spent the next eight years running away from Saul's attempts to kill him. David was anointed king over his own tribe of Judah at the age of thirty and was thirty-seven when he became king over a unified Israel. He reigned as king for a total of forty years (2 Samuel 5:3–5).

David was a bit of a renaissance man: shepherd, musician, loyal friend, compassionate leader, husband, father, warrior, protector, and a man after God's own heart (1 Samuel 13:14; Acts 13:22).

Hannah

She was the much loved and favored first wife (assumed) of a Levite named Elkanah who lived in the area of Ramah in the hill country of Ephraim. (Levites did not get their own territory but lived among the other tribes of Israel—Deuteronomy 18:1–8.) When Hannah proved to be barren, Elkanah married a second woman named Peninnah who bore him many children. Hannah was emotionally fragile; she was verbally abused by the second wife and desperate to have a child. She decided to pray for a son and vowed to give him into the Lord's service as a Nazarite. (See 1 Samuel 1:11; Numbers 6:1–5.) God granted Hannah's request and gave her a son for this purpose (1 Samuel 1:27–28). After Hannah followed through on her vow, God gave her five more children (1 Samuel 2:20–21).

Hophni and Phinehas

They were the worthless and evil sons of Eli who were priests (inherited position) but did not know the Lord personally. They abused and threatened the very people whom they were supposed to serve and represent to God. (See 1 Samuel 2:12–17, 22–25.)

Jonathan

The oldest son of Saul and at least twenty years old (legal fighting age) when Saul became king. He was a leader of men, brave, loyal, and kindhearted. He was married and a father of at least one surviving son, Mephibosheth (2 Samuel 9:6). Jonathan was probably at least thirty-five years old when he met David (approximately age fifteen), so their friendship was likely that of a *nice* older brother or mentor (very different from David's older brothers). Jonathan was levelheaded, a direct contrast to his father's mental instability. He was able to talk sense and calm Saul down but only for a little while. Jonathan was loyal to David until the day of his death at the hands of the Philistine army.

Family Drama

The book of First Samuel begins with the story of Hannah. She is the much loved (1:5) first wife of Elkanah who is in the priestly line of Kohath. Because she is barren (unable to have children), her husband has taken a second wife who bears Elkanah the sons he desires (1 Samuel 1:4). There are many issues represented in this first chapter, so let's take a closer look. Read 1 Samuel 1:1–8.

Barrenness and *sister wives*

What is the legal precedent? According to Old Testament law, a man was allowed to divorce his wife if she was barren, but many opted instead to add another wife who could give him heirs.[1]

What do Deuteronomy 21:15–17 and Mark 10:2–12 say on this topic?

Biblical examples of *sister wives*

Sarah and Hagar: Genesis 16:1–6, 21:1–10
Rachel and Leah: Genesis 29:30–30:2, 30:22–24
Hannah and Peninnah: 1 Samuel 1:1–8, 20–23

List the things that Sarah, Rachel, and Hannah have in common:

List the things that Hagar, Leah, and Peninnah have in common:

What do their husbands have in common?

Barrenness is not God's will. In Genesis 1:28 (KJV), "And God blessed them, (Adam and Eve) and God said unto them, Be fruitful, and multiply, and replenish the earth" (notation mine). In Genesis 9:1 (KJV), God repeated the instruction to "be fruitful, and multiply, and replenish the earth" to Noah. Psalm 113:9 (KJV) tells us that "He maketh the barren woman to keep house, and to be a joyful mother of children." This means that when you pray for the ability to bear children, you are praying according to God's will.

Bonus study: God alone opens and closes the womb

Genesis 20:17–18; 21:1–2; 29:31; 30:1–2, 22; Deuteronomy 7:13–14; 28:4,11; 30:9; Isaiah 66:9. It is interesting to note that God has special plans for firstborn sons all throughout the Bible—they are legally His (Exodus 13:2, 12).

Other barren women who had special firstborn sons

Rebekah: Take note that her husband, Isaac, prayed for her (Genesis 25:20–23).
Samson's mother, wife of Manoah: (Judges 13:2–24)
Elizabeth: Take note that her husband, Zacharias, prayed for her (Luke 1:5–13).

Warning about barrenness

We see the desperation in each of the barren women in this study that if left unchecked could have turned into bitterness against their husbands as well as God. It is vital to pray and trust God! (See Proverbs 30:15–16.)

Describe what Hannah's life was like sharing the house with Peninnah and her children. How did she cope with the abuse? (1 Samuel 1:6–7)

How would you feel if you were in her situation?

Satan Works through People to Steal Your Joy

What do you think of Hannah's solution to her problem? (1 Samuel 1:9-15)

Notice that there was a *lot* of emotion stirred up in this household. Peninnah was being mean to Hannah because her husband showed Hannah favor just like in Leah and Rachel's story. Hannah was withdrawing emotionally into herself and not eating. Elkanah was in the middle of the two women, feeling sorry for himself because Hannah didn't think that he was enough for her to love (1:8).

We are not told if Hannah asked Elkanah to pray for her or not. We saw in the example of Jacob and Rachel that a wife's desperation to have a child can put a lot of stress on a marriage (Genesis 30:1–

2). But we also saw the powerful result of a husband who is willing to pray for his wife's healing in Isaac and Rebekah's story (Genesis 25:21).

Do you think this example of a husband's prayer can be applied to a Christian couple who are dealing with infertility issues today? Why or why not? (James 5:16)

It's okay to feel sorry for Peninnah as well as Hannah. Her purpose in marriage was to bear Elkanah's sons who would inherit and carry on the family name and bloodline. She felt slighted by Elkanah's obvious preference for Hannah and acted out in the same way that Hagar and Leah did when they were treated in much the same fashion (Genesis 29–30). When you have love withheld from you, it is easy to take out your frustration on others and then feel superior in the one area of life where you are *better* than someone else. We can empathize with these women but also recognize that we can make better attitude choices and opt to make a better quality of life for ourselves and others who may be in a similar situation.

Read 1 Samuel 1:11 and 19–23 and Numbers 30:2–3 and 10–15. What vow did Hannah make and what did would it mean for the child himself?

The distance between Ramah and Shiloh was twelve to fifteen miles one way.

Hannah's vow didn't affect just her life but also that of her husband Elkanah. We are not told that she cleared it with him first or if he heard about the vow on the day she made it. Technically, Elkanah had the power to undo Hannah's vow, but according to 1 Samuel 1:23, he was trusting that it was of God and expected the Lord to confirm His word to Hannah. Have you ever made a vow/promise to God that someone else vetoed, or did they stand by your commitment? What happened next?

In my own life, I made a promise (vow) that if God would provide the money, I would donate it to the five different TV ministries that God was using to mature my faith. The money came from an unexpected source, and I praised God for the answer to my prayer. I wrote out the checks and had the envelopes addressed, stamped, and ready to mail, but when my husband discovered what I planned to do, he vetoed the plan. I had to trust that God saw my heart of obedience and that it was still His money to use for His purpose.

Later in the year, that money became the *seed money* to publish my first study guide: *12 Ordinary Men Who Lived Extraordinary Lives: A Study Guide on the Minor Prophets*. I believe that God was honored through my submission to my husband and enabled me to use the money for God's kingdom in a totally new way.

What does it say about Eli's personal thought life when he assumed Hannah to be drunk? (1 Samuel 1:9–18)

How do you think the actions of his sons with the women at the tent of meeting affected Eli's opinion of women like Hannah? (1 Samuel 2:22–24)

Have you ever been quick to judge others based upon your own bias? Was your opinion correct or way off base like Eli's?

What does 1 Samuel 1:17–18 say that shows Hannah had real faith in Eli's words?

Read Hebrews 11:1–3 and 2 Corinthians 1:20 and 5:7. What do these verses say our faith is to be based upon? What is it *not* based upon?

Bonus study on faith

Look up the definitions of the following: substance, hope, confidence, certainty, and expectation in the dictionary, then reread the passages above. How does it change your view of faith?

When Eli blessed Hannah, he was unaware that he was really blessing himself. Spread your words of blessing freely to others. You never know when they might come back to bless you in the future!

Read 1 Samuel 1:21–28 and Numbers 15:8–10. The weaning period for a child is anywhere from one to five years of age. I believe that Samuel was at least three years of age before Hannah brought him to serve in the temple because if he had not yet been able to eat regular food and be toilet trained, he would have been a burden to Eli and not any kind of help. The age of the sacrificial bull was three years, which may have been to match the age of the child who was Hannah's sacrificial gift to God. Also note that Hannah had to remind Eli who she was as it would have been four to five years between their initial conversation, conception, birth, and the weaning period. Hannah restates her vow in 1 Samuel 1:28.

Read 1 Samuel 2:18–21. How would you feel leaving your three- or four-year-old son in the care of an old man with the realization that you will only see your child once each year? What is your trust level in God's ability to care for your children when you aren't with them? Could you have honored the vow and made the sacrifice like Hannah did, never knowing if God will give you another child?

> *God often requires us to empty our hands*
> *before filling them with new things.*

Just like Jesus's mother, Mary, Hannah supported her son's service to God by helping to ensure that his physical needs were met. Our parental role changes from nurture and provision to emotional support and prayer as our children grow and mature in their personal walk with God. As parents, we must remember that ultimately our children belong to God. Our job is to train them in the knowledge and wisdom of God and then let them go to serve in whatever ways God may choose. (See Deuteronomy 11:18–21; Proverbs 22:6.)

1 Samuel 2:1–10 is Hannah's beautiful prayer of thanksgiving to God. Compare it with Mary's prayer in Luke 1:46–55 and Zacharias's prayer in Luke 1:67–79.

What do these prayers have in common?

How are these prayers different?

Samuel was an example of a man born to serve God all of his life. John the Baptist was another example of such a man, and, of course, Jesus is the ultimate example of a man born with one purpose—to serve God from birth to death. They all lived, served, and died in very small areas of Israel. Though their ministry lives remained close to the place of their birth, their sphere of influence was great, and the effects are still seen in the world today. Compare 1 Samuel 2:26 and Luke 1:80 and 2:52. What do these men's childhoods have in common?

Read 1 Samuel 2:12–17 and 22–25. What kind of men and priests were Hophni and Phinehas?

Bonus study

Who were the women who served at the doorway to the tent of meeting? (Exodus 38:8; Luke 2:36–38; 1 Timothy 5:5, 9–10)

It is sad to note that Hophni and Phinehas were married and had children of their own. They not only abused and mistreated the women who served at the tent of meeting but also did it in a very public way that humiliated their own families. Their sins adversely affected everyone who came there to worship God.

Read 1 Samuel 2:27–36 and 3:11–14. Who brought God's message to Eli?

Were the two messages the same?

Do you think that God had already tried to talk to Eli about his sons? Could it have been that Eli turned a deaf ear to God's gentle, private correction and therefore God brought others to speak a harsh, public correction?

What does 1 Samuel 2:29 say was Eli's main sin against God?

What was the generational curse on Eli's family line? (1 Samuel 2:30–33)

Four people in Eli's family died on the same day: the first victims of the curse (1 Samuel 4). How was the curse also fulfilled in 1 Kings 2:26–27?

Has there ever been a time when you have chosen *not* to hear what God was saying to you privately, and later God sent someone or something into your life that brought the same message but in a much harsher and public way?

What is the description in 1 Samuel 2:35 of the *one* God will raise up for Himself? Do you think this is talking about Samuel, Jesus, or both? (1 Samuel 3:19–21, Hebrews 2:17)

Read 1 Samuel 2:11, 18–20, 26, and 3:1. What do these verses say about Samuel and Eli's relationship?

Read 1 Samuel 3:2–21. Where did Samuel sleep?

According to Exodus 25:10–22 and 40:34–38 and Leviticus 16:2, what is so surprising about Samuel's sleeping arrangement?

Because of where Samuel slept, it's not surprising that he heard God's voice calling to him. What were the steps that Eli told Samuel to take to hear God's message?

1 Samuel 3:9, Lay down in _____

Today: Have a regular place to spend time with God each day.

1 Samuel 3:10, Speak, Lord, for Thy servant is

_____

Today: In prayer, allow time to be quiet and listen more than you talk.

1 Samuel 3:11, I am about to do a thing _____

_____

Today: Have an open mind to hear the big/new thing God wants to do

1 Samuel 3:18, Samuel told him _____ and hid _____ from him

Today: Speak the truth: God's message, *not* your interpretation of it.

1 Samuel 3:18, It is the Lord _____

_____

Today: Accept what God says and don't fight or rebel against it.

Notice that Samuel was afraid to obey God (tell Eli the message), but he did it anyway. Compare this to Ananias in Acts 9:10–17. How are these two calls of God similar?

Following the voice/message of God can be scary because we don't know what the outcome will be. It takes faith to believe that if we obey God's direction and speak His message; the results are up to God, and He will work it out for your good. It is also interesting that both Ananias and Samuel's messages came at night while they were on their beds (sleeping).

What reason does Job 33:15–18 give to explain God speaking to us during the night hours?

1 Samuel 3:19–21 tells us that Samuel *grew* in his walk with God, and none of the words that God gave him to speak *fell*. Because Samuel was faithful with the first words God gave, he proved that God could trust him with more until it was not only God's voice Samuel heard, but God revealed Himself (His heart, character, and presence) to Samuel.

Our life in Christ is called a walk for good reason. When we come to Jesus for salvation, we begin our Christian life as a *baby*; and as we learn and grow by reading, listening, and obeying the Word of God, we will grow and mature into the fullness of Christ. (See 1 Peter 2:2, Ephesians 4:13.)

It's important to remember that even Jesus had to grow in wisdom and stature and in favor with God and man (Luke 2:52 KJV). Don't get discouraged if you're having a hard time hearing and obeying God. Every walk with Jesus begins with a first step; if you aren't sure that you have a relationship with Jesus Christ, turn to the back of this study and take the step to make sure right now.

Read Ephesians 4. How is a person who is maturing in their walk with Jesus described in this chapter?

What are the areas where you see good growth in your life? What are the areas where you see little growth? Stop right now and ask the Holy Spirit to help you mature in these areas of your life.

The Loss of the Ark

The Promised Land of Israel is made up of mountains, foothills, valleys, and plains. In the books of Samuel, we will attempt to follow our characters as they move up and down from place to place on the map. Some of the locations no longer exist today, but many still can be found in Israel and the Middle East.

In the fourth chapter of First Samuel, we will focus on the Ark of the Covenant and what it meant to the nation of Israel as well as the Philistines who took it as a prize in battle. Read Exodus 25:10–22. How is the Ark of the Covenant described?

What was the importance of the "Mercy Seat" of God to the Israelites?

Bonus study on the "New Covenant"

Jesus is our access to the Mercy Seat of God (Hebrews 9:1–6, 11–15, and 10:19–22)

Read 1 Samuel 4:1–9. Did the people seek God's direction/ advice before going to war with the Philistines? What was the result?

> *The Philistines were around during at least one*
> *thousand years of Israel's history before this event.*
> *Their tactics were well known to Israel.*

What did the Elders decide they needed to do? (1 Samuel 4:3–9)

Who came with the ark and how did it get there?

How did the Israelites react?

How did the Philistines react?

Bonus study on Philistines amid one thousand years of Israel's history before David

Abraham: Genesis 21:22–34; Isaac: Genesis 26:1–31; Moses/Israel boundaries: Exodus 23:31–33; Joshua/Israeli army: Joshua 13:1–3; Samson: Judges 13–16

Read 1 Samuel 4:10–22. How many men of Israel died in the battle?

What does 1 Samuel 4:13 say that Eli was worried about?

From 1 Samuel 4:17–18, how does Eli's reaction to the news of his son's deaths compare to the news about the missing Ark of the Covenant?

How did Eli's daughter-in-law (Phinehas's wife) react to the same news in 1 Samuel 4:19–22?

Which part of the news concerned her the most?

What does this tell you about the importance of God's presence over any other human being in your life?

Have you ever lost someone in your family? How important was the presence of God to you at that moment?

Read chapters five and six of First Samuel and try to locate the Philistine cities you read about on a map located in the back of your Bible (some may not be shown). Remember that the war they fought with Israel took place in Aphek (twenty miles away from Shiloh, where the ark was taken from the tent of meeting, and Eli was anxiously waiting).

What did the Philistines do with the ark? (1 Samuel 5:1–2)

What took place during the night hours? (1 Samuel 5:3–5)

Bonus study on Philistine's idol: Dagon the fish/man

Joshua 19:27 (beth = house + Dagon); Judges 16:20–30; 1 Chronicles 10:7–10

What physical reaction to the ark did the Philistine people experience? (1 Samuel 5:6)

What did the people of Ashdod decide to do? (1 Samuel 5:6–8)

Gath was the city where Goliath's family lived (giants). What happened to the men in the city when the ark was brought to stay? (1 Samuel 5:9)

What did the people of Ekron do when they saw the ark coming? (1 Samuel 5:10–12)

Where does it say the "cry of the city" went to?

How long was the Ark of the Covenant in the hands of the Philistines? (1 Samuel 6:1)

Maybe you are amazed how long it took for the Philistines to wise up and give the ark back to Israel, but how long do you put up with the negative results of your sin before you are willing to let go of it and return to God? Notice that the Philistines knew they were guilty before Israel's God. In 1 Samuel 6:6, what event did they compare it to?

Isn't it interesting that the heathen gentile nations knew all about Israel's history in Egypt and the power of their God in rescuing them from slavery? What advice did the heathen priest/diviners give to the Philistine leaders about the ark? (1 Samuel 6:2–9)

Note what form the Philistines guilt offerings took. They made their offerings to God in the shape of the very things God had used to bring His judgment upon them: tumors and rats. It seems strange, but when I thought about how to apply this to my life, I considered how the very things that God puts His finger on and tells me to get rid of because they are hurting/hindering me are the same things that I offer back to Him in the sacrifice of obedience.

For example, when God told me that I was spending too much time with books and TV shows, which were polluting my mind and harming my spiritual walk, I repented and sacrificed those same things back to Him. I sold the books and used the money to buy Bible-based books that would help me in my Christian walk, and I stopped watching *worldly* TV shows and watched Christian TV shows instead.

Is there anything in your life that you need to repent of and offer back to God as a sacrifice of obedience?

What was the significance of using two milking cows, which had just given birth to calves as the means to pull the cart carrying the ark?

What does 1 Samuel 6:9 say about their reasoning?

What did the cows do? (1 Samuel 6:12)

Ekron to Beth Shemesh was a journey of approximately eight miles. According to 1 Samuel 6:13–16, how did the people of Beth Shemesh react when they saw the ark approaching? (Beth Shemesh was a Levitical city: Joshua 21:8–16.)

What happened to the people who peeked at the contents of the ark? (1 Samuel 6:19)

Why did it happen? (Numbers 4:17–20)

The number of fifty-thousand and seventy men given in 1 Samuel 6:19 is thought by some to be an error made by the man copying the text. Hebrew texts use the word for seventy, and the other older documents show the number written as seventy men.[1] The Tree of Life Version of the Holy Scripture (translated by Jewish believers) of 1 Samuel 6:19 states that seventy out of fifty thousand men were struck down.[2] It is probable that these men were not descendants of Aaron as they showed no fear or respect for the ark as the seat of God's presence and power.

What was the reaction of Beth Shemesh's residents to the men's deaths? (1 Samuel 6:20–21)

> *The ark became a "hot potato" that no one wanted to catch!*

Samuel's Ministry Begins

We have read about the capture of the Ark of the Covenant and the damage it caused to those who didn't respect the power and presence of God that resided with the ark. Now we will find out the next stage of the ark's journey back to Israel.

Read 1 Samuel 7:1–6. Where did the ark end up? For how long?

The territory of Kiriath-Jearim (also known as Baale-Judah—2 Samuel 6:2) was located on the border between Judah and Benjamin. See if you can find it on the map in your Bible. Even though it was not a Levitical city, Abinadab and his sons are thought to have been Levites. It is interesting that God allowed Eleazar to serve in the role of priest for twenty years without any negative effects, but his brother could not say the same. Read what happened in 2 Samuel 6:3–8 when Eleazar's brothers Uzzah and Ahio were chosen to help King David in his first attempt to move the ark to Jerusalem.

In Samuel's role as Israel's priest, what did he tell the people to do? (1 Samuel 7:3–6)

Ashtaroth/Asherim (plural) Ashtoreth/Asherah (singular)

The female god of Sidon was Baal's wife and mother goddess. She had different names, depending on the nation: Ishtar, Babylon; Astarte,

Greek and Roman.[1] *Asherah poles were made of wood or stone that represented a female body and were worshipped through prostitution (1 Kings 14:23–24).*

Temples to Baal and Ashtareth are usually found together. (See Judges 6:25.) The worship was through orgies of pleasure (food and sex). Baal was an idol that looked like a bull. (The golden calf that the Israelites made in the wilderness is an example; Exodus 32:1–4.) He was considered to be the god of fertility, rain, greed, and success.[2]

This idol is still worshipped *today in New York. The bronze sculpture of a bull was placed on Wall Street in 1989. It was made by Sicilian sculptor Arturo Di Modica, following the 1987 "Black Monday" stock market crash.*[3] *3*

Read 1 Samuel 7:5–14. The Philistine nation was constantly looking for a fight with Israel, so when they heard that there was a large gathering at Mizpah, they showed up for war. How many leaders of the Philistines were there, and what major cities did they represent? (1 Samuel 6:16–18)

How did the Lord respond to the people's fasting, repentance, and the offerings burnt on the altar by Samuel? (1 Samuel 7:5–12)

Bonus study: final destruction of Philistia

Jeremiah 47; Isaiah 14:28–32; Ezekiel 25:15–17; Amos 1:6–8; Zephaniah 2:4–7; Zechariah 9:1–7

What did Samuel do to commemorate Israel's victory? (1 Samuel 7:12)

Many times throughout the Old Testament, we find followers of God setting up stones or physical reminders of the activity of God in their lives. Just as it was then, it is still important to have some kind of marker in your life today—a sign of the victory God has given you. When you are tempted to go back to old sins, you can look at them and remind yourself of God's goodness in saving you from that sinful way of life.

Bonus study: markers of God's activity/presence

Genesis 28:10–22, 35:9–15; Deuteronomy 27:2–8; Joshua 4:1–9

Read 1 Samuel 7:15–17. As a judge, Samuel had a regular circuit route that he would take every year. Notice that since the ark was no longer kept in Shiloh (where the tent of meeting was still set up), Samuel used his home in Ramah as the base of his ministry. It's interesting to note that Bethel, Gilgal, and Mizpah are all located in the territory of Benjamin where the best warriors lived. The first two kings of Israel had to be warriors because they were still surrounded by nations that were at war with them. (Solomon was the first king to have peace on all of his borders; 1 Chronicles 22:9.)

See if you can locate these cities on your Bible's map.

> *Bethel*—located five miles north of Ramah. Founded by Jacob after he had the dream about the ladder with angels going up and down to heaven (Genesis 28:10–22).
> *Gilgal*—located ten miles northeast of Ramah where Saul was made king (1 Samuel 11:14–15).

Mizpah—located three miles northwest of Ramah. This is where Samuel chose Saul to be king by casting lots (1 Samuel 10:17–24).

As a circuit judge, Samuel made civil (legal) and religious (sin) judgments for all Israel. Just as the people would line up outside of Moses's tent in the desert to be judged (Exodus 18:13, 16–22), if the elders of a city could not decide a legal matter, they would wait until Samuel visited and let him make the decision.

Read 1 Samuel 8:1–3. Here, we meet the two sons of Samuel: Joel and Abijah. These men were at least thirty years old (Numbers 4:2–3) and married with children. Samuel's family was from the Levitical line of Kohath (1 Chronicles 6:33–34.)

How are Samuel's sons Joel and Abijah described?

Bonus study: Kohath line and their role in serving God

Numbers 4:1–20; 1 Chronicles 6:31–38. Haman the singer is Samuel's grandson via Joel. He played with the musicians in the *parade* when David brought the ark of God to Jerusalem. (See 1 Chronicles 15:16–19.)

Why do you think that Eli and Samuel (highly respected priests in Israel) both had sons who had no fear of God like their fathers had?

What does this tell you (if anything) about their parenting skills?

It's sad, but this problem still exists today. Many children of pastors and missionaries turn *away* from God instead of *to* the God of their parents. It is important to remember that serving the Lord well begins by serving our own families well. How do Deuteronomy 11:18–21 and Proverbs 22:6 tell us to raise our children, and what is the promise in these verses?

Notice that it was Samuel who appointed his sons to the role of judge. Both Joel and Abijah served in Beersheba, which was located at the extreme southern territory of Israel, approximately forty-eight miles south of Jerusalem and even farther away from their father's home in Ramah. See if you can locate the city on a map in the back of your Bible.

Read 1 Samuel 8:4–9. How many elders came to talk to Samuel? (Remember that there are actually thirteen different familial tribes in Israel—Joseph's sons Ephraim and Manasseh count as one in the listing of twelve). What were the elders' complaint, their request, and their reasoning?

This is a big problem in our lives today. Followers of Jesus are *supposed to be different* from the world around them instead of down-playing the holy standards of God and trying to fit in with their environment. We are to be light in a dark world and salt to a tasteless generation. (See Matthew 5:13–16.) Those who adopt the world's standards and yet consider themselves Christians should wonder if they are truly saved or not. (See Matthew 7:21 and Philippians 2:12–16.)

For example, How holy are you in your choices of TV shows, movies, websites, music, video games, and the like? Would you want Jesus to be sitting next to you? Wake up! The Holy Spirit is present with a believer at *all* times!

What was Samuel's reaction to the elder's comments in 1 Samuel 8:6?

Do you think he had personal feelings of rejection as well as on behalf of God?

Read 1 Samuel 8:7–22. For over three hundred fifty years, judges had ruled Israel and been the voice of God to the people. Now the people were rejecting not only the position of a judge but also *especially* Samuel's sons in that role.

What was the Lord's response to Samuel?

It is possible that Samuel felt guilt over the actions of his sons; their actions were bad enough that *all* of the elders of Israel had to come talk to him. Wasn't it kind of God to reassure Samuel that the people weren't rejecting him personally?

Samuel held the roles of priest, prophet, and judge for the majority of his life, so it must have been hard to let go of a position that had become such a large part of who he was. Who would he be without it? What would his life look like now? According to Numbers 4:2–3, priests could only serve to the age of fifty, so his sons had already taken over that role. To give up the role of judge would leave Samuel *only* the role of prophet.

Even though Samuel's sons were a terrible family legacy, he did leave a legacy of *spiritual sons* who would stand in the role as prophets to the nation of Israel. During Samuel's ministry, he set up prophet schools for young Levites to train them how to hear God's voice just as Eli had trained him. These prophet schools are mentioned all throughout the book of Samuel and also mentioned in the days of Elijah and Elisha in the book of Kings.

Bonus study: schools of the prophets

1 Samuel 10:5–6, 10–11, and 19:18–24; 1 Kings 18:4 and 13; and 2 Kings 2:2–7, 15–18, 4:1, 6:1–7, and 9:1–10

Was God surprised by the people's request for a king? Read Deuteronomy 17:14–17, which was written about three hundred years before this event took place. Read 1 Kings 10:26–29 and 11:1–13. Notice that it was David's son Solomon who did everything that God said *not* to do, and his descendants paid the price. What did the Lord say the king would *take* from the people in the verses below?

1 Samuel 8:11–12 (This was prophetic since Israel didn't have these items at this time.)

1 Samuel 8:13

1 Samuel 8:14

1 Samuel 8:15

1 Samuel 8:16

1 Samuel 8:17

According to 1 Samuel 8:18, what will be the response of the people to the king's demands?

What will be the Lord's response?

People who reject God in the good times of life have no right to expect His help and protection when bad times come. When an individual or nation rejects God, they have chosen to move out from under God's hand of protection, and therefore, they will experience the direct results of their choice (sowing and reaping—see Galatians 6:7–8).

The sons of Eli and Samuel were raised in the temple by fathers who served the Lord, but somehow, the faith of their fathers did not reach down into the lives of the sons. These sons held positions in the temple but had no personal relationship with God themselves. Believing that God exists is not enough. It is only the first step; even the demons believe in God. Faith without correlating action is not true faith (James 2:14–20). God says to be holy as He is holy; if our belief is real, it must show up in our daily choices. (See Leviticus 11:44a and 1 Peter 1:14–19.)

How many people today are attending and possibly serving in a church and consider themselves to be Christians, but they have no real personal relationship with Jesus Christ? As Joyce Meyer says, sitting in a garage does not make you a car, and sitting in a pew does not make you a Christian. [4] To be a Christian, a person must be a follower of Christ, a disciple of the Son of God, who died, came back to life, rose from the tomb, and went back to heaven and is sitting at the right hand of the Father. Jesus is coming back soon, and this time, He will come in the role of judge (Matthew 25:31–46).

It has been said that God does not have any grandchildren. Each and every person must make their own, individual choice to accept Jesus as their *personal* savior, believe that He died for them, and then choose to receive His payment for their sins. It doesn't matter what your parents or grandparents did in service to God, you must make your *own* choice to believe and follow Jesus. It says in Romans 10:9–10 (KJV),

> That if thou shalt confess with thy mouth the Lord Jesus, and shalt believe in thine heart that God hath raised him from the dead, thou shalt be saved. For with the heart man believeth unto righteousness; and with the mouth confession is made unto salvation.

If you're not sure that you have asked Jesus to be your Savior, please stop right now and turn to the page at the end of this guide for more Scriptures and instructions on how you can begin a relationship with Jesus today.

For those of you who are in a personal relationship with Jesus and have a longstanding ministry for the Lord, how is your family doing? Are your children following the Lord? Consider how you might feel if you were asked to step down from your position/ministry. Would you be able to let it go and trust that God has something different/better in mind for you and for the place you serve? Would you keep a good attitude or complain and grow bitter?

It is important to remember that God often asks us to let go of the *old thing* in order to have empty hands to receive the *new thing* that He has for us. (See Philippians 3:13–14). What are you holding on to that God has already told you to let go of? Are you willing to let go today?

The Making of a King: Saul

The story of Saul begins like many good stories. Once upon a time, there was a man named Kish whose donkeys had run away. He decided to send his oldest son on a quest to find the missing animals. This son was tall and handsome, and he fearlessly set off on a long journey. Along the way, he met a strange man who told him amazing things. The awesome truth is that this story really happened, and if you are a follower of Jesus, you can also live an amazing adventure!

Read 1 Samuel 9:1–2, 10:23–24, 13:1, and 14:47–52. How do these verses describe Saul?

In contrast to other translations such as NASB and NIV, the Tree of Life Version of the Holy Scriptures translation (TLV) of 1 Samuel 13:1 states that Saul was thirty years old when he became king, and he reigned forty-two years. [1] If that is true, then there must be a gap of many years between Saul's anointing by Samuel and the war he fought with the Philistines. Saul put Jonathan in charge of men, which means he had to be at least twenty years of age. (See Numbers 1:45.) Either way, we will study later that Saul died after a battle against the Philistines at the age of seventy-two.

Read 1 Samuel 9:21, 10:22, 13:11–12, 14:24, 15:19–21, and 30. What do these verses reveal about the *inner character* of Saul that people could *not* see?

Bonus study: warrior tribe of Benjamin

Genesis 49:27; Judges 3:15–28 and 20:15–16; and 1 Chronicles 7:6–12, 8:40, and 12:1–2. Sin of Benjamin: the men of Gibeah and Saul's family line. Judges 19:16–21:24

When reading the Bible, we should put ourselves into the story in order to better understand the real-life person who lived it. Read 1 Samuel 9:3–5. What was Saul doing before he met Samuel?

Saul lived in Gibeah. His search took him east and west through all of Benjamin's territory and finally north into the hill country of Ephraim in the land of Zuph (1 Samuel 1:1) where Ramah (Samuel's home) was located. The trip was long enough that Saul thought his father would become more worried about his life than the welfare of the missing donkeys.

What was the servant's advice to Saul? Read 1 Samuel 9:6–14.

Notice that God sent people across Saul's path just when he needed direction/information to take the next step. God will do the same thing in your life today. Pray for God's favor and that you would have eyes to see and ears to hear what your next step should be. (See Isaiah 30:20–21.)

On Samuel's side of the encounter, he knew that God would provide Israel a king, but he didn't' know who or when it would be. Samuel didn't have to go looking for a man to be king. God brought the man to him. He had probably been praying about it, and in 1 Samuel 9:15–17, we read God's answer to Samuel's prayer.

When did Samuel hear about Saul, and what was he told?

The New Testament calls this message a word of knowledge, *one of the gifts of the Holy Spirit found in 1 Corinthians 12:8. Don Stewart gives this definition: "The gift of the word of knowledge refers to the ability to know facts about a situation or a spiritual principle that could not have been known by natural means. This allows someone to see a situation as God sees it."*[2]

Read the rest of Saul's encounter with Samuel in 1 Samuel 9:17–10:13. Notice all the details we are given:

> Worship together at the high place
> Special seat of honor in the midst of thirty other men
> Special portion of food at the meal that had been reserved just for Saul
> Spent the night in Samuel's own home

Samuel put Saul's mind at rest about the donkeys with the information he had received from another *word of knowledge.* After all this special treatment, Saul must have been confused about what was really happening. He was forty years old, married with kids, and working for his father. Now this strange prophet was pouring oil on his head and telling him that God had chosen him to rule over all Israel. Samuel also told Saul that he would encounter several things on his trip home. List the things that would happen:

1 Samuel 10:2

1 Samuel 10:3–4

1 Samuel 10:5–6

What does 1 Samuel 10:7 say these events were for?

What does 1 Samuel 10:9 say happened to Saul *internally?*

What does 1 Samuel 10:10–13 say happened to Saul *externally?*

Compare Saul's experience to what Peter said happened in Acts 2:15–18 and 33.

God does not change. He is the same yesterday, today, and forever (Malachi 3:6; Hebrews 13:8). The gifts of the Spirit are for *all* who believe in Jesus as Lord and Savior—that includes you! (See 1 Corinthians 12:3–11.) How exciting and radically changed would our lives be if all of God's people would be led by the Spirit as we go about our daily lives, interacting with people who need to hear from God?

In 1 Samuel 10:8, Samuel told Saul to meet him at the town of Gilgal in seven days and that Saul should not do anything before Samuel arrived. Read 1 Samuel 10:14–16.

As soon as Saul arrived back in Gibeah, his uncle Ner (Abner's father) started questioning him about what Samuel had said. (The servant must have told Ner that Samuel had asked to speak to Saul privately.)

Why do you think Saul didn't tell his uncle the whole truth?

Both Saul and Samuel knew that the Lord had chosen Saul to become king over Israel, but they needed to go through a public process to prove it to the rest of the people so that the decision could not be disputed later if/when Saul proved to be an unpopular leader.

Read 1 Samuel 10:17–27. The city of Mizpah was located approximately seven miles north of Jerusalem within a few miles of Gibeah where Saul lived. (See if you can locate it on the map in the back of your Bible.) Samuel called all of Israel together and began by reminding the people that in choosing to have a king like the surrounding nations, they were rejecting God as their king.

How did Samuel get his information on God's choice? (1 Samuel 10:20–21)

Compare his actions to Joshua 7:14.

Which of the twelve tribes was chosen? (1Samuel 10:20)

Which family line was chosen? (1 Samuel 10:21)

Which person in the family was chosen? (1 Samuel 10:21)

Why did they have to ask the Lord where Saul was? (1 Samuel 10:21)

Bonus study on casting lots

Psalm 22:18; Proverbs 16:33 and 18:18; Leviticus 16:8; Numbers 26:55 and 33:54; Joshua 18:8–10; 1 Samuel 14:41–42; Esther 3:7; 1 Chronicles 24:5; Nehemiah 10:34; Jonah 1:7; John 19:23–24; and Acts 1:26 (last time mentioned in the Bible)

Casting lots was like throwing dice—believing that the number/ symbols would direct the next steps/actions to take. The apostles, disciples, and believers that made up the new church in the first century, as well as followers of Jesus today, do not need to cast lots because the Holy Spirit lives inside of us. He will direct our next steps if we ask and take the time to listen for His answer. (See Psalm 37:23–24; Isaiah 30:20–21.)

What does it tell you about Saul's (thirty-/forty-year-old) character that he was hiding behind some baggage while people were yelling his name and looking around for him? Crouched with his head down among the pack animals? (1 Samuel 10:22–23)

Do you think Samuel said these words with a straight face, or was he being a little bit sarcastic? (1 Samuel 10:24)

Read 1 Samuel 10:25–27. After Samuel reminded the people of all that the king would require of them (1 Samuel 8:11–17), he wrote all the ordinances in a book and placed it before the Lord. Samuel dismissed the people, and everyone went back to their homes to wait and see what would happen next. How do you think their lives would change under a king compared to being under God's leadership?

I am writing this book during an election year, and today is the day we will hear who our next president will be. Which do you prefer to rule your life? A man you can see or a God that you cannot? Do you see any parallels to your own life situation right now? Is God on the *throne* of your life or are you? What do the following Scriptures say about our invisible God?

John 1:18 and 14:7–9

Romans 1:20

Hebrews 11:1–3

Saul went back to his family home in Gibeah, but this time, he was surrounded by men whose hearts God had touched to serve their new king (his new bodyguards and the beginnings of an army). There were obviously some worthless men who didn't agree with God's choice of Saul. They questioned his ability to deliver them from their enemies. We are told that they despised him and didn't bring him any presents. Saul was told about these men or maybe even heard their words himself, but he chose not to say anything to defend himself. These might be the very same worthless men who try to stir up trouble for David later in 1 Samuel 30:22.

Have you ever had to defend yourself against others' negative opinions of you and/or the position of authority that God has placed you in? Have you ever made negative comments about the president of your country? Those in leadership positions in your own life: employer, pastor, parent, governor? Besides being an election year while I am writing this study guide, it is also the year of COVID-19 (2020).

It is amazing to hear the words coming out of the mouths of people who call themselves Christian. It is hard to tell them apart from the world's loud voices on the TV, radio, and Internet. This should not be! God's people are called to be salt and light in the earth, not to be chameleons that conform their external views to match the world around them.

What was your reaction during the last political campaign in your country? What words did you speak about the candidate you didn't like? What was your reaction to your state or country COVID-19 mandates to *shelter in place* for months and months? What words came out of your mouth then?

What do the following Scriptures say about our words?

Proverbs 18:21

Matthew 12:34–37

James 3:8–10

What is in your heart and mind will come out of your mouth! Be careful!

Write out Psalm 141:3 and memorize it this week.

Saul's Early Years as King

Soon after Saul had returned home to Gibeah with his new army of valiant men, he received a distress call from the elders of Jabesh-Gilead. Look at a map in the back of your Bible to locate these two cities as well as Bezek where the army met up. (Jabesh-Gilead is sixty to seventy miles east of Gibeah, and Bezek is about seventeen miles northeast of Shechem.)

Read 1 Samuel 11:1–13. What was the problem?

> *The loss of a right eye would restrict most fighters,*
> *but if he was left-handed, his shield would be*
> *in the right hand protecting his right eye.*

How did the people of Gibeah feel about the plight of Jabesh-Gilead, and what was their response? (1 Samuel 11:4)

What was Saul doing when he heard what the messenger told the people? (1 Samuel 11:5)

Saul may have been a king in name, but as yet he was still acting as a farmer working in the family fields. He doesn't seem to have any plans to actually set up a kingdom. What happened when the Spirit of God came upon Saul? (1 Samuel 11:6)

How did Saul send a message to all the tribes of Israel? (1 Samuel 11:7)

Compare his actions to those found in Judges 19:29–20:9.

Do you think Saul sent the message this way because he was from the very town mentioned in the previous Scripture from Judges?

How did the people react to Saul's message in 1 Samuel 11:7?

God is never late, but He is rarely early either. Waiting for God's answer to our prayers stretches and strengthens our faith "muscles." When we wait for God's timing, we can be confident it will result in the best outcome.

Remember that the men of Jabesh-Gilead only had seven days to send for help and for help arrive in time to save them. Seventy miles is a long way to hike and then fight a war, so Saul first traveled to the city of Bezek. There he was joined by three hundred thousand men of Israel and Judah's thirty thousand fighting men (twenty years and older). Bezek was on the west side of the Jordan River and Jabesh-Gilead on the east side. This meant that they probably crossed the river in the middle of the night in order to arrive in secret. They set out on a three-pronged attack during the morning watch (3:00 a.m. to 6:00 a.m.)

What happened to the army of Ammon? (1 Samuel 11:11)

The people were so excited by Saul's first big victory against their enemies that they wanted to punish the men who had disagreed with God's choice of king. What was Saul's response, and who did Saul say delivered Israel? (1 Samuel 11:12–13)

The problem of Jabesh-Gilead was the instigating event that caused Saul to let go of his old life (farming) and step fully into the new role (king) that God had called him to. Is there any area in your life that God has told you to let go of so that you can step into the new thing that He has planned for you to do?

If you remember, Samuel had anointed Saul in private (10:1), and at Mizpah, he told the people all the ordinances (rules) of how the new kingdom would work (10:25) and wrote them down in a book. In 1 Samuel 11:14–15, Samuel gathers all the people back to Gilgal to reaffirm Saul as king. This time they did it before the Lord and offered sacrifices and peace offerings in an official ceremony.

Why was the town of Gilgal so important? Read Joshua 4:19 through 5:2–9.

Gilgal was the place where Israel originally set up an altar and remade their covenant of circumcision. The word *Gilgal* means *rolling*. Joshua said it was the place where Israel's past status as slaves in Egypt rolled off of them, and they were now fully God's people.

First Samuel chapter 12 is Samuel's retirement speech to all of Israel. How does Samuel describe himself? (1 Samuel 12:1–3)

Did the people agree with his statements? (1 Samuel 12:4–5)

What times in their history did Samuel remind them about? (1 Samuel 12:8–12)

What are the "if...then" statements in 1 Samuel 12:14–15?

If:

Then:

Do you think Samuel was still mad at the people and that's why he called down thunder and rain on their ripe crops or was it to remind the people of God's power over their lives? (1 Samuel 12:17–18)

Bonus study: The voice of God through nature

Job 37; Exodus 19:16; 2 Samuel 22:14–15; Psalm 18:9–15 and 29:1–11; Jeremiah 10:13 and 51:16; John 12:28–29; Acts 9:3–7; Revelation 6:1, 8:5, 10:3–4, 11:19, 14:2, and 19:6

What is the final warning Samuel gives the people in 1 Samuel 12:21–25?

What does Samuel promise to continue doing on their behalf even after he has retired from his role as judge? (1 Samuel 12:23)

Samuel's instruction in 1 Samuel 12:24 is still true for us today. *Fear God* (worship and respect His power), *serve God* all of your heart (commit to Jesus as Lord of your life), and remember the great things God has done for you (*thank God*).

Bonus study: What's so special about the men of Jabesh-Gilead?

Read ahead to 1 Samuel 31:8–13 to see how long their loyalty to King Saul lasted. See what King David promised them in 2 Samuel 2:4–7 to reward their loyalty.

Saul the Warrior King

First Samuel chapters 13–15 cover events during the first twenty years of Saul's reign. We are told that Saul fought the Philistines all during his life (14:52) as well as other surrounding nations such as the Ammonites, Amalekites, and Moab (14:47–48); so these chapters are *only a sampling of battles* that took place during Saul's first twenty years as king of Israel. Wars with the Philistines were ongoing, and cities were taken and retaken throughout Israel's history. (Compare 1 Samuel 13:2–3 to 13:5 and 16.)

War over the ownership of cities and territories is still going on today in Israel.

Read 1 Samuel 13. The chapter begins by telling us Saul's age at the beginning of his reign (forty) and the length of his reign: thirty-two years. Saul has assembled an army, which is made up of four thousand men whom he split into different units. Saul leads one, and his oldest son Jonathan (at least twenty years old at this time) leads the other. We aren't told in what year of his reign this battle took place, but in 1 Samuel 13:1 (KJV) it says that Saul reigned one year; and then in his second year, he gathered men (including Jonathan) for an army to fight against the Philistines.

Jonathan started the fight by attacking a Philistine garrison in Geba. The rest of the Philistine army heard about the battle and brought thirty thousand chariots, six thousand horsemen, and an unnumbered army of foot soldiers to fight Israel (1 Samuel 13:5). Saul saw this huge army and knew that his own army of four thousand men would not be enough. He summoned all Israel's men of fighting age to Gilgal to assemble for battle. The Israelis who lived in the war zone were so afraid that they left their homes and hid out in caves, cliffs, cellars, pits, and some even left the region and crossed over the Jordan River to Gad's territory (1 Samuel 13:7). They obviously thought Saul's army had *no* chance.

In 1 Samuel 13:8, Saul is waiting at Gilgal for Samuel to arrive and give God's instructions for the battle. (Compare with 1 Samuel 10:8.) But Saul became impatient waiting. When Samuel was late, Saul took over the position of priest and made the sacrifices himself (1 Samuel 13:8–9).

What was Samuel's response? (1 Samuel 13:10–14)

Who did Saul blame? (1 Samuel 13:11–12)

The *"blame game" began in the Garden of Eden* (Genesis 3:11–13).

Do you think God's decision was too harsh for first-time disobedience, or do you think the reason is found in 1 Samuel 13:13–14?

How is the *next* ruler of Israel described?

1 Samuel 13:19–22 gives us more background information about the weapons the men of Israel had to fight with. What does this tell you about the average Israeli soldier?

Bonus study: How God uses confusion to win over the enemy

Genesis 11:7–9; Exodus 14:23–25 and 23:27; Deuteronomy 7:1–23; Joshua 10:7–10; and 1 Samuel 14:19–20

What do you learn about the character/personality of Saul's oldest son, Jonathan, from reading 1 Samuel 14?

What does the reaction of his armor-bearer tell you about Jonathan's leadership skills?

God moved on Israel's behalf only *after* Jonathan stepped out in faith. God helped Jonathan and his servant defeat twenty men and then sent an earthquake to create confusion among the entire Philistine army. They scattered and became easy targets for Saul's army to catch and kill.

The great-grandson of Eli (Ichabod's nephew, 1 Samuel 4:21), Ahijah, was serving Saul as a priest with the ark of the Lord in the army camp (1 Samuel 14:3, 18.) When the earthquake happened in 1 Samuel 14:15, Saul took it as a sign from God that something important was happening and asked Ahijah to find out what was going on (by casting lots). The only problem was that there was no time to do it. God intervened and caused confusion. The people had

SAUL THE WARRIOR KING

the Philistines on the run, and Saul had to join in. Even the people who had previously hidden out in caves joined in the chase, and the Lord delivered them.

What was the problem in 1 Samuel 14:24, and who caused it?

What is wrong with Saul's avenging statement in 1 Samuel 14:24?

By Saul's use of "I," "myself," and "my," we understand that his focus was not on God or even the people; it was all about Saul. The heart attitude that God had seen was now obvious for all to see.

What is the difference between these statements and the comment Saul made in 1 Samuel 11:13?

Look up Luke 6:45. How does this verse apply to Saul?

How can you apply Luke 6:45 to your life?

What natural food provision had God provided to the tired and hungry people? (1 Samuel 14:25–26)

What is so amazing about where they found the honey?

How is this similar to the manna that God provided for His hungry people every morning in the wilderness? (See Exodus 16:13–15, 21, 31)

We are told in 1 Samuel 14:27 that Jonathan had not heard his father's statement (curse). What was his response when he was told? (1 Samuel 14:29–30)

Do you think Jonathan was disloyal to his father (the king) by stating his opinion to others? Why or why not?

In 1 Samuel 14:31–34, what was the result of Saul's curse? (What did the people do when the fighting was over, and they were tired and hungry?)

Read Leviticus 17:13–14. What was the law that the people were breaking?

It's hard to be patient, kind, gentle, loving, and self-controlled (fruits of the Spirit in Galatians 5:22–23) when we are tired and hungry. Satan knows that this is when we are the most vulnerable. Study his attacks on Jesus in Luke 4:1–13.

What does Luke 4:13 say that Satan waits for?

What does 1 Peter 5:8 say about Satan's attacks?

Stay alert and the lion *can't* eat you. Satan *only* has the power you *give* him.

Saul got the bright idea that his army should raid the Philistine camp that same night. The Israelites were tired from fighting all day and now had full bellies. The priest stopped Saul and suggested they should first ask God whether or not this was a good idea.

What happened next? (1 Samuel 14:36–46)

Do you think curses still exist today? Why or why not?

According to Galatians 3:10–14 and Romans 5:12–21, does God's grace through the blood of Jesus take care of any curse/law of destruction?

God removes every curse and replaces it with His blessing. Write out God's blessing found in Numbers 6:24–26.

Jonathan readily admitted to his father what he had done (the people already knew). He was willing to die, and Saul was ready to kill him, but the people wouldn't allow it. They said that it was evident that Jonathan was blessed by God because he had brought them victory in battle. Anyone that God is blessing should not be put to death for such a (dumb) reason as Saul's emotionally based curse.

First Samuel 14 ends with more historical information about Saul. He was married and, at this time, had three sons and two daughters by his wife Ahinoam. Do you find it surprising that Saul chose his cousin Abner to be the captain of his army? David also chose family members to lead his army; Joab, Abishai, and Asahel were his nephews (1 Chronicles 2:16).

Read all of 1 Samuel 15. This was Saul's last chance to prove that he was a willing and obedient servant of the Lord, but he failed. When Samuel arrived, he reminded Saul that he was king *only* because God had given him the position, and God would be the one to take it away. Who did God want Saul to fight, and what was the reason? (1 Samuel 15:2–3)

Bonus study: God versus Amalek

Who were they? (Genesis 36:12) Famous battle: (Exodus 17:8–13) What did God swear to do? (Exodus 17:14–16) What was God's instruction? (Deuteronomy 25:19)

Why does God want Saul to use such extreme measures against the Amalekites? (1 Samuel 15:3) Compare Saul's instructions to Moses's found in Deuteronomy 20:16–18.

Compare Saul's disobedience to Joshua's obedience in Joshua 11:8–15. What did Joshua do that Saul did not?

Who were the Kenites? (1 Samuel 15:6) See Judges 1:16 and Exodus 18:6–12.

The Lord gave the Israelites victory over the Amalekites. God did His part, but did Saul do his part? What did Saul *not* do? (1 Samuel 15:9)

Partial Obedience = Disobedience

What happened in 1 Samuel 15:10–11? Was Samuel at the battlefield with Saul?

This is another example of a *word of knowledge;* God told Samuel about Saul's disobedience and His regret at making Saul king of Israel. What was Samuel's reaction?

What did Saul do at the city of Carmel that proved to Samuel and the people that his heart was not toward God? (1 Samuel 15:12)

What was Saul's response when Samuel confronted his disobedience? (1 Samuel 15:13–23)

Who did Saul put the blame onto this time? (1 Samuel 15:21, 24)

Saul forfeited the good plan God had for his life. His disobedience affected not only his family but all of Israel also. If it was true that Saul allowed himself to be pressured by the people's desires (wanting to keep the spoil for themselves) and not at his own direction, then he proved himself a poor leader. Anyone in a leadership role (boss, teacher, parent, pastor, and the like) is answerable first to God, then to others.

How do you respond to God's correction in your life? Do you *own* your actions/decisions, or do you blame others? Do you *cry out* to God in distress, guilt, and shame, or do you *agree* with God (confess) and *accept* the grace of God through the finished work of Jesus on the cross and *move on* with your day?

Bonus study: What God does with our sins?

Psalm 103:12; Isaiah 1:18; Micah 7:19; Ephesians 2:8–9; Hebrews 8:12 and 10:17–18; and 1 John 1:9

In 1 Samuel 15:22–23, Samuel reveals the heart of God about sin. What are the comparisons Samuel uses in these verses?

Burnt offerings/sacrifices are less important than_____.

Heeding (listening/obeying) is better than_____ _____.

Rebellion is equal to the sin of _____ _____. (See Deuteronomy 18:10–12.)

Insubordination is equal to the sin of_____
_____.

In 1 Samuel 15:24–27 and 30, we see that even though Saul finally agreed with Samuel and confessed he had sinned (compared to 15:20), his heart was not changed. Saul still cared more about what the people thought of him than what God thought about him. How does this apply to your life today? Do you care more about how many *likes* you get or how many followers you have on your internet sites than what God thinks about what you say and do?

1 Samuel 15:29 is a well-known verse that can be somewhat confusing. Keep in mind 1 Samuel 15:11; God regretted making Saul king. In Genesis 6:6, God regretted and was sorry that man was wicked and must be destroyed. God often regrets man's actions, and therefore, God's necessary response to man must change to reflect His discipline. God's *character, who* He is: He *is love.* He *is mercy.* He *is good.* He *is righteous.* He *never* changes.

Agag thought he was not going to be punished for his actions against Israel, but Samuel did what Saul was unwilling to do; killing Agag was messy and harsh, but he fully followed God's instructions (1 Samuel 15:32–33). What does Galatians 6:7–10 say we can expect to be the outcome of our actions?

King Agag had an *infamous* descendant named Haman who also tried to exterminate the Israelite nation (Esther 3). If Saul had fully obeyed, perhaps Haman would never have been born.

1 Samuel 15:35 ends with a confusing statement. It says that Samuel did not see Saul again until the day of his death. This could be Samuel's literal death, or at the time Saul called a dead Samuel up from Sheol through the medium in 1 Samuel 28:3–25. Either way, we are told in 1 Samuel 19:19–24 that at a later date (when Saul was chasing after David), Saul was in Samuel's presence at the prophet

school in Ramah. It is possible that 1 Samuel 15:35 is out of order of the actual timeline of events, or it is a prophetic statement for Saul's future.

David Enters the Scene

Samuel spent a lot of time and effort teaching Saul how to conduct himself as a king should: obedient to God's directions and putting the people's needs above his own. Saul proved to lack integrity and cared more about his own ego and what others thought of him than meeting the needs of God's people. He was *not* a good shepherd! (John 10:11–13)

Samuel was emotionally hurt and disappointed over Saul's rebellion against God. He may have had a little *pity party* because in 1 Samuel 16:1, God gave Samuel a verbal "kick in the pants" to get him to stop looking back at the door God had closed on Saul's kingship. It was time to walk through the new door of opportunity that God was preparing for David.

Grief is a process, not an event; it's not completed in one moment, one day, one month, or even one year. We aren't told how much time God gave Samuel to mourn and let go of the dream/vision he had for Israel's future. But God knows that if grief goes on for too long, it can become something else entirely. What do these verses tell us about grief?

Psalm 34:18

Isaiah 53:4

2 Corinthians 1:3–5

> God knows we need time to grieve.
> He will help us to let go and move on.

Remember that God often requires us to let go of the old thing in our life in order to have room to accept the new thing He has for our future. Has there ever been a time in your life when God closed a door, and you had a hard time letting go of the person, place, or thing?

What *word of knowledge* did God give Samuel about His new choice of king? (1 Samuel 16:1–13)

Why was Samuel afraid to go to Bethlehem?

Fear Is the Foundation of All Lies

Notice that Samuel asked God for a creative idea of what to say to Saul if/when he was questioned. Samuel didn't want to lie. So many people in this book of First Samuel chose *not* to ask God for help and simply lied to save themselves. God cannot and will not bless a lie, but if we ask Him for help, He will give us a creative way out of the situation and still tell the truth. What do these Scriptures say on this subject?

Psalm 34:11–17

Proverbs 3:21–26

Matthew 10:16–20

Luke 12:11–12

James 1:5

Why were the town elders afraid of Samuel? (The answer may be found in 1 Samuel 12:18)

How many sons did Jesse have?

If David was the baby of the family, he was the tenth child of Jesse. Besides having seven older brothers, David also had two older sisters (1 Chronicles 2:13–16). David was born *after* Saul became king of Israel, so he was in his mid-teens at this point in time. We know that at least three of David's brothers were old enough to fight in Saul's army (1 Samuel 17:13). To have seven grown men ahead of him in birth order, the oldest brothers were probably at least in their mid-thirties. Unlike Joseph and his father Jacob's close relationship, Jesse didn't give David any special treatment; if anything, David seemed to be ignored by his father.

According to Jewish tradition, David's mother was named Nitzeret. In an article by Chana Weisberg, she reports that some Jewish traditions say that David was thought to be the illegitimate child of his mother (not the son of Jesse), and this was the reason David was treated as a servant more than a son or brother.[1]

I encourage you to read this article in its entirety because it shows that David was *not* illegitimate; he only appeared to be through a strange set of circumstances. This is much like Jesus and His mother Mary's situation. There were those who whispered that Jesus was illegitimate due to the unique and *unbelievable* true story of His birth. We know that David was the true son of Jesse because God was careful to preserve the bloodline of Jesus in order that all messianic prophecies might be fulfilled. Read Isaiah 11:1–5 where the Messiah is prophesied to be the root of Jesse.

Jesus truly was the Son of David whose bloodline goes all the way back to Adam, the first son of God. Read Luke 3:23–38 to see Mary's side of the bloodline, which comes through David's son Nathan. Mary's husband Joseph's bloodline is found in Matthew 1:1–17. It begins with Abraham, not Adam, and comes through Solomon.

Look up Psalms 51:5 to read what David said about his mother and how he was conceived. Do you think David believed he was illegitimate?

David may have felt insecure because of the questions surrounding his birth. Throughout the book of First Samuel, he calls himself a dead dog. Because of the lack of his father's attention, he learned early in his life to depend upon God while he tended the sheep. (See Psalm 23.) In 2 Samuel 7:18–22, David acknowledged that his life and all he had were supplied by God alone.

Read Psalm 139 to see what God said about David and about you! Which of these verses will you take as your own encouragement today?

Read 1 Samuel 16:6–13 and 17:12–29 and put yourself in the brother's place and think about their reactions to David's anointing. Compare David's experience to Joseph and his brothers in Genesis 37:2–19.

David

Joseph

How would you react if you weren't chosen to do great things and your little brother was?

Samuel remembered how tall Saul was, and what a fine physical image he brought to the position of a king so he looked favorably upon David's older brothers.

What did God tell Samuel He was *not* looking for? (1 Samuel 16:7)

What does God see that we cannot?

You'll notice that Samuel did not cast lots to find out which of Jesse's sons God had chosen to be the next king of Israel. This time, God wanted Samuel to look and listen with the eyes and ears of his heart (the Holy Spirit). God didn't tell him the man's name, age, or physical description. Sometimes God purposefully doesn't give us all the information we want or require in a situation. He wants us to stay in tune with the Spirit and listen for His guidance. If we go into situations thinking we know exactly what will happen, we are not walking by faith, and we may run ahead of God's purpose and plan, or we may miss it altogether.

What did Samuel do when none of the men was the one God wanted for the job? (1 Samuel 16:11)

Samuel could have thought that he had misunderstood God, but instead, he asked for more information and discovered the direction that God intended him to go. Samuel made the men stand around waiting for David to be brought in from the fields. They were not allowed to go into the feast until God's chosen man was anointed and given the place of honor just like Saul in 1 Samuel 9:22–24. Samuel didn't make any judgments based upon David's appearance or age even though he was used to basing a man's eligibility to serve God on his being physically perfect. (See Leviticus 21:17–23.)

God likes to do new and unexpected things. (See Isaiah 43:18–19 and Habakkuk 1:5.) God looked at David's heart, not his height or physical strength. Samuel simply obeyed God and anointed a handsome young man to be the next king of Israel, and his act of obedience was validated when he saw that the Spirit of the Lord came mightily upon David from that day forward (1 Samuel 16:13).

We aren't told that David began to prophesy when the Spirit came upon him, but since that is what happened to Saul, it is safe to assume that there was some kind of outward sign given. We are told that Samuel went home to Ramah and did not attempt to train David as he had with Saul. Samuel understood that God was done with Saul, but David could not be openly groomed to rule as long as Saul was alive. As it turned out, Samuel died before David ever took the throne.

The biggest difference between Saul and David was not their age or physical appearance; it was their heart. David had the heart of a shepherd and learned at a young age to care for the needs of others before his own. He went without sleep; he saw to the sheep's need for food and water; he cared for the sick and risked his own life to protect theirs. God's own heart is the heart of a shepherd, and this is why God calls David a man after His own heart. (See 2 Chronicles 16:9a; 1 Samuel 13:14; Matthew 5:8; John 10:11–15, 21:15–17.)

Bonus study: God chooses to use shepherds

Abel, Genesis 4:2–4; *Jacob and sons,* Genesis 30:31–43 and 37:12–16; *Moses,* Exodus 3:1, 4:2, and 17; *David,* 1 Samuel 16:11, 19, 17:15, 20, and 28; *King Cyrus,* Isaiah 44:28 and Ezra 1:1–4; *Amos,* Amos 1:1 and 7:14–15; *Shepherds in the field,* Luke 2:8–20; *Jesus,* Isaiah 40:10–11, John 10:11–16, and 1 Peter 2:25; *Peter,* John 21:15–17; *Church elders,* 1 Peter 5:1–4

Throughout ancient history, shepherds were often looked down upon and treated as the lowest social caste. (See Genesis 46:33–34.) Jacob became a shepherd for his uncle because he was a thief and swindler who ran away from his father (in shame) and his brother (in fear for his life) to hide among his mother's relatives. Moses was a murderer hiding in the wilderness from the wrath of his adoptive grandfather, Pharaoh. (It's amazing how alike Jacob and Moses met their wives!) Whether or not David was considered illegitimate, he was put out in the wilderness, out of sight and out of mind from the daily interactions of his family.

Historical legend told by Greek Historian Herodotus says that *King Cyrus's* life was in danger as a child (from his grandfather); he was taken in by a shepherd and lived with the family for the first ten years of his life.[2] *Amos* was a shepherd, taken from his own lands and commanded by God to speak the terrible visions of God's coming judgment. *Angels* first appeared to lowly shepherds out in the fields of Bethlehem to announce the birth of the Messiah. *Jesus* left heaven to become our "Good Shepherd." Jesus commissioned *Peter* to be a shepherd over the church that was coming soon, and called *elders* to be shepherds over the believers in their churches. God loves to use shepherds, but all of these men also had to learn the lessons of the wilderness before they were *ready* to fulfil the plan God had for their lives.

No One Is Too Low or Unimportant for God to Use

Read 1 Samuel 16:14–23. David is still a teenager, living at home and continuing to shepherd his father's sheep. The Holy Spirit of the Lord has left Saul, and God's power and hand of protection have been removed. We have already seen that even *with* the presence of the Holy Spirit, Saul had mental and emotional issues dealing with his own self-image. When God's presence was removed, Saul was left with only his own tormenting thoughts. The statement in 1 Samuel 16:14, "an evil spirit from the Lord," can be confusing.

Look up 2 Chronicles 18:18–22. What does this example tell you about this spirit?

The word angel *means "messenger." God's heavenly angels do not deceive or lie. They represent God in whom there is no darkness (1 John 1:5). God did not send an angel to deceive Saul; it was an evil spirit (following Satan's leadership: John 8:44; Revelation 12:9–10) who magnified the fear that already filled Saul's mind and used it to torment him. It was Saul's acts of disobedience that opened the door to this spirit (1 Samuel 15:23; Ephesians 4:20–27).*

Read James 1:12–17. What do these verses say about the character of God and man's inclination to sin?

Bonus study: Does God change?

Compare Malachi 3:6; 1 Samuel 15:29; Numbers 23:19; Genesis 18:17–33; Exodus 32:9–14; Jeremiah 26:13 and 19; and Jonah 3:9–10, 4:2, and 11

Why did Jesse have to obey Saul's request? (1 Samuel 8:11, 17)

What did Jesse send along with David? (1 Samuel 16:20)

How did Saul feel about David, and what was his position in the household? (1 Samuel 16:21–23)

Saul's *love* of David was based upon what David could do for him unlike the love of Jonathan, which thought of what he could do for David. It's often been said that love and hate are two sides of the same coin, and it has now been confirmed by science. Scientists have found that in the brain, emotions of hate use the same nervous system circuits as emotions of love.[3]

It is important to notice that the evil spirit attacking Saul's mind had to shut up in the presence of the Holy Spirit who was upon David. The book of Psalms is full of the songs written by David, so it's a good chance that he was singing and playing songs of worship and praise to God while in Saul's presence.

Evil cannot stay in the presence of worship.

There seems to be a time jump of several years from 1 Samuel 16–17. Saul no longer knows or recognizes David (1 Samuel 17:55–58). David is probably now in his late teens, so it could be that after serving as Saul's musician for a year, he was allowed to return home to serve his father in the sheep fields. Considering how much a teenage boy can grow and fill out physically in his late teens, it's not all that surprising that Saul didn't recognize David as the boy who had played music for him years earlier.

1 Samuel 17 is probably one of the most well-known stories of the Bible; as you read it, remember that David was a real person. Put yourself in his sandals as you read this real-life event. The story begins on the battlefield in the Valley of Elah; the Philistines have set up across the valley on the hillside opposite of the Israeli army. For forty days, they have been taunting Israel trying to get the war started.

Describe the Philistine's champion: Goliath. (1 Samuel 17:4–7)

A cubit equaled the length of a man's forearm, approximately eighteen inches. A span was considered to be the width of a man's stretched-out hand (pinky finger to thumb), which equaled about nine inches or one-half of a cubit. This means that Goliath was approximately nine feet nine inches tall.[4] The giants who lived in Gath were thought to be descendants of Anak, a tall race mentioned in Numbers 13:33; Deuteronomy 1:28 and 9:1–2; and Joshua 11:21–22.

What did Goliath say to the Israelite army? (1 Samuel 17:8–10)

What were Saul and his army's reaction? (1 Samuel 17:11)

The narrator's *voice* in 1 Samuel 17:12–14 speaks as if we don't know who David is. This may mean that this story was written by a different author (Gad or Nathan) from the earlier chapters which were probably written by Samuel.

Just like today, many parents use their younger children as message carriers between themselves and others. David's father, Jesse, wanted to know how his three older sons were doing in the war, so he sent David with supplies of food, not only for his sons; but also for the commander of their unit. Read 1 Samuel 17:12–19.

What supplies did David bring with him? (1 Samuel 17:17–18)

The number forty in the Bible is almost always used in connection with times of wilderness, dryness, or testing. Goliath called out twice a day for forty days; the rain lasted forty days and forty nights to flood the earth; the children of Israel wandered in the desert forty years; Moses was on the mountain with God for two sets of forty days; and Jesus was tested in the wilderness forty days.

Interesting fact. The Latin meaning of the word *quarantine* is "forty days of isolation."[5] My year of writing this lesson during a quarantine has been a time of separation and testing not just for me but for the entire world as well.

David was a curious teenager who wasn't yet old enough to fight (younger than twenty), so he was probably happy to go to the battlefield and see what was happening. Read 1 Samuel 17:20–31. What questions did David ask?

Who did he ask?

What did his oldest brother think of David's questions?

Do you think Eliab was jealous of David (anointed to be king) or merely afraid to look bad in front of the other soldiers?

David's brother Eliab may have treated him horribly because he thought he was illegitimate or just because David was the baby of the family. Compare Eliab's comments/emotions (17:28–29) with those of Joseph's brothers when Jacob sent Joseph to check on them in Genesis 37:2–20. (Joseph wasn't anointed but he did have a dream.)

What was Saul's reaction to David's offer to fight Goliath? (1 Samuel 17:31–37)

> *Letting David meet Goliath as Israel's champion was a huge risk. If David had lost, Israel would have become servant to the Philistines.*

How did Saul try to help David prepare for the battle? Did it work? (1 Samuel 17:38–39)

What was David's special skill set? (1 Samuel 17:34–37)

God will often use your *natural talents* in your area of service to Him.

What *tools* did David take with him and why? (1 Samuel 17:40)

How do David's shepherd experiences and his tools compare to those of Jesus in Psalms 23 and John 10:11–15?

What was Goliath's reaction to David with his staff and sling? (1 Samuel 17:41–44)

God's rod and staff bring Christ's followers comfort because He uses them to defend us from those who try to harm us (Psalm 23:4b).

Which of the well-known words that David spoke to Goliath bring you the most encouragement for your life situations today? (1 Samuel 17:45–47)

Remember that faith is activated when you speak it out loud in words! God formed everything you see in this world by the words of His mouth. (See Genesis 1 and Psalm 33:6–9.) How do the following Scriptures compare with David's prophetic, faith-filled words?

Mark 11:22–23

Luke 6:45

2 Corinthians 4:13 and 18

How did David approach the battle lines? (1 Samuel 17:48)

Saul and the entire Israeli army were afraid of giants just as their forefathers were when Moses led them to the edge of the Promised Land. At that time, only Caleb and Joshua were ready to run to the battle line and take the land God had promised. The other ten men talked negatively about the giants they had seen, and the more they talked, the more people became afraid. Because they feared giants more than they believed God, they turned back to wander in the desert until all of the men (besides Joshua and Caleb) died in the wilderness (Numbers 13). In the end, Caleb did fight the giants to get his own land (Joshua 14:6–15). This time when the Israeli army faced a giant, God spoke to the heart of the one man who wouldn't listen to the voices of fear and doubt, but who would run to the battle even if no one else followed him!

If you stare at the giant in your life (problem) long enough, you will end up talking yourself and others out of following the direction God has given you. If God has told you to run to the battle line, there is an anointing on you to do it; but if you stand around talking about the problem, the anointed window of opportunity will pass. Satan loves to talk and will make sure that you hear lots of negative voices to keep you from stepping out in faith!

Do you see the importance of David running to the attack? Goliath had no time to lift his shield to protect his head (defense) or to throw his spear (offense). His pride made him a sitting duck for David's stone. According to 1 Samuel 17:49–50, David's stone hit Goliath in just the right place (either between the eyes into the brain or on the temple at the side of his head), killing him instantly and knocking him to the ground where David could reach him. 1 Samuel 17:51 tells us that David cut off Goliath's head with Goliath's own sword. This was to prove (to both armies) that Goliath was really dead and not just unconscious. What happened next? (1 Samuel 17:51–53)

1 Samuel 17:54 informs us that David brought Goliath's head to Jerusalem. It is said that he buried it on a hill outside the city; a place that in Jesus's day was called *Golgotha: the place of the skull.*[6] The place of memorial to David's victory against Israel's enemy became the same site of Jesus Christ's (the *Son of David;* Matthew 1:1) victory over mankind's enemy (the devil). Through His crucifixion on that hill, Jesus became not only the Savior of Israel but also the Savior of the entire world (John 3:14–17).

In 1 Samuel 17:55–58, it reiterates that Saul had forgotten who David was but because of his bravery; Saul commandeered David into service in his army. I believe this proves that several years had passed since David served as Saul's page and court musician. David was nearing twenty years of age and legally eligible to serve (1 Samuel 18:5).

How can you apply this story to your life? Has God ever asked you to do something bigger than you thought possible? Did other people try to tell you how to accomplish it? Did you try to do it their way, or did the Holy Spirit use the gifts God had already placed inside of you to accomplish it?

It's important to remember that when you serve the Lord Jesus Christ, you do so with the gifts and talents that the Holy Spirit has given you. No one can do what you can do in the same way that you can do it. It's important to follow the leadership of the Spirit within you rather than the opinions of those who may want to help you accomplish a task. Their input may get in the way of God's plan for your life if it is not godly counsel.

Do you allow your feelings to get hurt or offended if/when someone in a position of authority forgets your name or the previous times you have served in the ministry?

What does God say about offense?

Proverbs 19:11

Romans 12:16–18

1 Corinthians 13:4–7

What is done in God's time,

in God's way,

in God's strength,

will always end in victory.

David and Jonathan

When I was in Sunday school classes, as a child, the teachers would often tell the story of David and Jonathan's friendship. The pictures used to tell the story always portrayed them as young men of the same age, height, build, and so forth. I guess no one ever stopped to read the surrounding Scriptures to figure out that David wasn't yet born when Saul became king. Since Jonathan was a leader in Saul's army, it means that he was at least twenty years of age during the first years of Saul's reign. Therefore, Jonathan was probably twenty years older than David (approximately thirty-five years old when he met David).

Read 1 Samuel 18:1–4. Who was the instigator of the friendship?

What type of love did Jonathan have for David?

What do these Scriptures say about this type of love?
John 13:34–35 and 15:12–13

DAVID AND JONATHAN

Romans 13:8

Philippians 2:1–4

What did Jonathan give to David proving his commitment to their covenant? (1 Samuel 18:4)

We read in 1 Samuel 13:19–22 that only Saul and Jonathan had actual weapons. What do you think it meant for Jonathan to give up these items to David? Remember that Jonathan was Saul's oldest son and expected to inherit the throne.

Everything that Jonathan gave David belonged to a royal heir, everything that David would need to lead a nation into war. It was a visual sign of Jonathan's support and authority. Do you think God had already told him that David would be the next king, or do you think David told Jonathan about Samuel's anointing?

Read 1 Samuel 18:5–30. I believe verses 6 through 9 prove that several years pass and many wars take place during this time period. Saul set David over part of the army, and even though he was still in his early twenties, all the people respect him (1 Samuel 18:30). Saul didn't like David getting so much attention, and soon all of his *love* turned into jealousy, fear, anger, and then hate.

Where did Jonathan's loyalty lie? With David or his father the king? (1 Samuel 19:1–7)

How did Jonathan show David his loyalty?

What was Saul's reaction to Jonathan's rebuke and counsel? (1 Samuel 19:4–6)

Read all of 1 Samuel 20. Saul made multiple attempts to kill David in person and also hoped that by sending David to war with the Philistines, they would kill David for him, but David continued to have success, and Saul was desperate. He began using his own soldiers to pursue David, men who had served beside and followed David into battle. Jonathan learned of Saul's plan and was anxious to protect David from his father's assassins.

What were the questions David asked Jonathan? (1 Samuel 20:1)

When things seem to be going wrong in our lives, it is wise to ask God these same questions in case we have sinned and need to repent. These questions can be a good test of the intentions of our hearts that become the foundation of our actions.

How did David describe his situation in 1 Samuel 20:3?

What word does David use to describe himself in comparison to Jonathan's princely position? (1 Samuel 20:7–8)

What legal term did David use to describe his friendship with Jonathan? (Note that it was at Jonathan's instigation) (1 Samuel 20:8)

This agreement was not just between the two men. God was a part of this contract. Marriage vows are another example of a covenant made between two people but spoken before God and other witnesses. God is always the third party to any covenant that we make. Ecclesiastes 4:12 says that it is the third strand that gives strength to the rope, and in the same way, it is God who gives the strength to any promise or covenant we make with another person.

How does this compare to God's covenant with His people in Jeremiah 31:33–34?

What plan did they come up with so David would know if it was safe to be in public again? (1 Samuel 20:9–13 and 18–23), and what was the result of the plan? (1 Samuel 20:24–40)

What parts of the covenant between them did Jonathan want to reaffirm? (1 Samuel 20:14–17 and 41–42)

God often places people in our lives for future purposes we have no knowledge of at the time. It was God who gave David favor with the older Jonathan. It was Jonathan who instigated the covenant with David, and God used their friendship as a shield to protect David from Saul's manic, life-threatening jealousy. The covenant also protected Jonathan's son and grandson yet to be born. (You can read 2 Samuel: 9:1–13 and 21:1–7 to see how David kept his part of the covenant with Jonathan.)

This story shows the importance of asking God for the right friendships in your life. Ask God to give you favor and deep connections with other believers, especially those who are more mature in their walk with the Lord. It is also important to hold all of your friendship/relationships with open hands. You must allow God to move people in and to move people out of your life, trusting Him to know the right timing of these relationships in any given season of your life.

Have you ever experienced a deep connection of favor with another believer?

Have you ever had a hard time accepting it when God moved you out of a close relationship?

In the New Testament, we have an example of Paul, Barnabas, and a young man named John Mark (Acts 12:12) who went together on a mission trip but for reasons unknown. John Mark left the others and went back home early (Acts 13:1–13). Paul and Barnabas completed the trip, but later, when it was time for another mission trip, Paul refused to allow John Mark to come along. This caused a quarrel between Paul and Barnabas, and the result of the quarrel was that they split off from each other, and their names are never seen paired again in the Scripture (Acts 15:36–40).

Paul went on to travel with others, and so did Barnabas, but they had to let go of each other in order to move into other seasons of service. It's interesting to note that years later, Paul specifically asked for John Mark to come visit him in prison because he was such a help to him. (See 2 Timothy 4:9–11.) God may bring past relationships back around in future seasons, so always leave others with words of blessing and honor. Did you know that John Mark is the author of the Gospel of Mark in the New Testament? God can and will use us no matter how or where we start from.

Barnabas was a Levite, and his *real* name was Joseph. It was the apostles of the early church who gave him the new name of Barnabas, which means "son of encouragement" (Acts 4:36). Just like Jonathan, God used Barnabas to help, protect, and encourage a younger man on his journey to follow God.

Is there anyone from a younger generation in your life that you could encourage in their journey with God?

This week, pray and ask the Holy Spirit to put someone in your path that you can encourage.

People Who Protected David

God and Satan both work through regular people. Satan was using Saul and his army to take the life of David (God's anointed), but at the same time, God was utilizing different people to protect David from Saul and his assassins. Satan's goal is always to kill, steal, and destroy (John 10:10). God's plan is always to prosper you and not to harm you, to give you a future and a hope (Jeremiah 29:11).

If Saul had been successful in killing David, Jesus would never have been born.

God will always send people/information to help you in your time of need. Your part is to pray, ask for help, listen to wisdom, and trust God *while you obey* what He tells you to do. We saw from our previous study the deep connection that Jonathan had with David.

How did God use *Jonathan* to protect David in these Scriptures? 1 Samuel 19:1–7

1 Samuel 20:1–2 and 25–42

In 1 Samuel 18:17–29, we read how Saul gave his younger daughter, Michal, to be David's wife in the hope that she would become a snare to David (distraction) so that he might be killed in war with the Philistines. Saul's plan did not work; instead, how did *Michal* protect David? (1 Samuel 19:11–17)

During this time period, the prophet Samuel had retired and lived at his home in Ramah. How was *Samuel* used to protect David? (1 Samuel 19:18–24)

What did *Ahimelech*, the priest of God, do to help David that made Saul angry enough to order him and his family killed? (1 Samuel 21:1–9, 22:9–20)

Believe it or not, David was so desperate to get away from Saul that he left the territories of Israel and went to *Achish*, the Philistine king of Gath to hide. The very city that Goliath was from!

Read 1 Samuel 21:10–15. How did David get away without being harmed?

God will help us think creatively when under pressure if we ask Him. Read what David had to say about this event in Psalm 34. How does David describe *God's* protection, and what promises can a believer claim for themselves today?

Do you see in this Psalm how David approached God in prayer? Find the phrases which demonstrate each of these categories:

Praise and worship:

Stating the problem/situation:

God's answer:

David's testimony/praise report:

Read 1 Samuel 22:1–4. As we saw with Ahimelech, anyone who helped David was considered to have committed treason. In the "Background of the Book of First Samuel" section of this study, we learned that David's great-grandmother, Ruth, was from the country of Moab. It is possible David still had relatives there and felt that his parents would be safe to stay with the *king of Moab* while David himself was on the run. David left his parents in Moab, but we can assume that by this time, his older brothers had joined David's army and were on the run with him.

What warning did the prophet *Gad* give to David in 1 Samuel 22:5?

Even though Saul agreed at two different times that he would no longer chase after David (see 1 Samuel 24:16–22 and 26:17–25), David didn't really believe it. So he went again to live among the Philistines, to *Achish* the king. Some scholars suggest that Achish welcomed David because he was now seen as a traitor in Israel, and with his personal army of six hundred men, he would be considered a possible ally. Saul finally stopped searching for David once he permanently moved out of Israel's territory.

Read 1 Samuel 27 to 28:2. How did Achish honor David?

Do you think David was right to lie to Achish about his raiding activities? Why or why not?

Do you think that David's lies were okay with God? Why or why not?

Compare David's raiding activities to the events found in 1 Samuel 30:1–14. Do you think God allowed David to experience the same fear, pain, loss, and damage that he had caused to others by his actions? (Galatians 6:7, principle of sowing and reaping)

God was gracious and allowed David to recover everyone and everything that had been taken from him and his men. Hopefully, David learned to have more empathy and gained wisdom for future decisions—decisions that would affect many thousands of God's people, not just his army and his personal household.

Has there ever been a time in your life when someone else protected you from harm? Looking back, can you see how it was God who moved that person to protect you?

I have many memories of times when God's love and mercy protected my life. Most of them were during my teenage years when my stupid actions/choices *deserved* bad results, but God's grace saved me from any real harm (Ephesians 2:4–5). God gave me these words to speak whenever situations arise that bring fear:

God is good, and *everything* He does is good and for my good.

I encourage you to ask God for a verse that you can speak over your life when you are fearful or in need of protection. The words of the Holy Spirit are life and peace (Romans 8:6).

David's Life on the Run from Saul

Read 1 Samuel 18:5–9 and 30. After David had served as a commander in the army, as well as Saul's personal musician for several years, Saul's feelings of jealousy, fear, and anger turned into hate. His mind became set on getting rid of David permanently. Notice the progression of Saul's sin. He began by looking at David with suspicion (evil thoughts), and the very *next day*, the evil spirit came upon him (1 Samuel 18:9–10).

It's important to remember while reading the following Scriptures, for most of this time, David was running, not just with his army of four hundred men but all of their wives and children too. As we already studied, anyone who helped David was considered to be a traitor to Saul's government. David was on the run from Saul for six to eight years. (David was approximately twenty-two years old when married to Michal and thirty years old when the tribe of Judah anointed him king in 2 Samuel 5:4–5.)

Follow the route David took to get away from Saul by locating the places mentioned on a map in the back of your Bible. Note where he goes, how long he stays there (if given), and how God saves him in each place. Also note that many of David's Psalms were written during these years on the run.

Read 1 Samuel 18:10–11. How many times does it say David escaped?

What reasons do 1 Samuel 18:12, 15, and 28–30 give for Saul's desire to kill David?

Wisdom always brings respect when it is applied serving others.

Read 1 Samuel 19:1 and 9–10. Notice how many times David kept going back into service to Saul in the hope that there would be a different outcome. Do you think he is being stupid or just submissive and loyal to the authority that God has put in place?

Because David's own family tended to treat him badly, David may have been conditioned to consider Saul's cruel treatment as normal or to be expected. We know that David called himself a flea and a dead dog in comparison to Saul (1 Samuel 24:14). It's very easy to judge others' actions when we don't know the circumstances in which they have been raised. Thankfully, it is *not* our place to judge; *only God knows the why behind people's actions.* What is your reaction when a person in authority treats you badly?

Read 1 Samuel 19:11–12 to see how David escaped, and then read Psalm 59. In this Psalm, David reveals his thoughts and feelings about the event. How does David describe his enemies?

What does David want God to do to them?

What does David say that he will do?

It's easy to doubt and question the promise God has given you if/when things go wrong in your life. Saul's first tactic was to send other people to harm David (1 Samuel 19:15 and 20–21), but we see in 1 Samuel 19:18 that David escaped and fled to the one man who could confirm who David really was—God's anointed one and under His protection. Samuel was probably seventy to eighty years old at this time, and yet he encouraged David by traveling with him to *Naioth's* school of the prophets instead of staying at his own home in Ramah.

Has there ever been a time in your life when you felt like God promised you something good, and you got really excited, but then time passed, and maybe some bad things started happening that caused you to doubt you had heard from God?

David lived approximately fifteen years from when Samuel anointed him to be king until he actually became king (of Judah), and half of those years were spent running for his life. That's enough to make anyone doubt God's call on their life. Take courage and do what David did—seek God and ask Him to confirm His Word to you. He will guide you to Scriptures and/or send word through another person, a song on the radio, and so on. God is very creative in getting His Word to us when we are in need of hearing His voice. Take the time right now to ask God to confirm His call and direction on your life.

Read 1 Samuel 20:1–3, 30–33, and 42. We are told that after spending time with Samuel, David left Naioth and went to find Jonathan in *Gibeah* (his other source of encouragement). Because of helping David, Jonathan also came under physical danger from his father, Saul. What kind of friend are you? Has pressure from others ever caused you to turn away from helping a friend in need?

We just read about the physical and emotional cost Jonathan paid to be David's friend. Read 1 Samuel 21:1–9. It was David's lie that ultimately sealed the fate of Ahimelech and his family.

Read Psalm 52. David wrote this Psalm to express his anger at Doeg who killed all but one of Ahimelech's family members. Do you find it ironic that the first four verses of Psalm 52 talk about the sin of lying and deceit?

How do you think David has the confidence to say Psalm 52:8–9?

Read 1 Samuel 22:11-23. Doeg was an Edomite, which means that he was from the lineage of Esau. Edomites were cousins of the Israelites (Jacob's descendants), but they were always at odds with each other. (The story of Jacob and Esau is in Genesis 27.) Doeg had no fear of God when he killed the priests and their families. We see that Saul also has no respect for God's representatives or of God Himself. He continued to sink lower into evil thoughts and deeds, but notice that Saul's servants feared God more than they feared Saul.

You should notice a big difference in character between David and Saul in this story. Instead of blaming the deaths of Ahimelech and his family on Saul or Doeg. David places the blame on himself. It was his lie that opened the door for Saul to act so violently against innocent people, and he knew it. He made atonement for his sin by protecting Ahimelech's grandson who escaped the slaughter.

Have you ever lied to save yourself but then found that it cost someone else to suffer in your place? How did it make you feel?

David was under the law and had to make restitution for his guilt (Leviticus 6:1–7). Thank God that today believers are under grace, and Jesus has made our restitution for us! (Hebrews 9:11–14)

We read in 1 Samuel 21:10–15 that David next ran to the Philistines, King Achish of *Gath*, for protection. When the king's servants started asking questions, David came up with a creative plan to act insane and escape. From our earlier reading of Psalm 34:4, I think that the idea to act crazy came from God.

Next, David ran from Gath and hid in the caves of *Adullam*, a distance of ten to twelve miles (1 Samuel 22:1–2). This location is where all the other Israelites who didn't like Saul's leadership gathered to David. His family members also came to escape Saul's retribution for treasonous acts (being related to David).

David then traveled to *Moab*, which was located on the other side of the Dead Sea to drop off his parents as we already studied. After the prophet Gad warned David to leave the stronghold at Moab, he went to the *forest of Hereth*, which was near the caves of Adullam where he had previously hidden (1 Samuel 22:5). This is the first time that the prophet Gad has been mentioned. He may have just turned thirty years of age (old enough to serve) and been sent by God to travel with David. David kept Gad with him after he became king of all Israel (see 2 Samuel 24:11–14) so Gad would have firsthand knowledge to write down the events in these last chapters of First Samuel and into Second Samuel (1 Chronicles 29:29).

Read 1 Samuel 23:1–13. David heard that the Philistines (not king Achish) were attacking the city of *Keilah* to the south of where David was hiding in the forest of Hereth. David asked the Lord if he should go and fight them. God said yes, but the men of his army (grown from four hundred to six hundred) were afraid and didn't believe that David had heard God correctly, so David asked the Lord again, getting the same answer.

Have there been times in your life when you've prayed and felt like you heard from the Lord and knew what you were supposed to do next, but when you told other people, they brought fear and doubt into your mind? What did you do?

In Hebrews 11:1, we are told that faith is seeing through the eyes of hope without seeing any natural evidence. David had a long history of hearing God and not only believing what he was told but then acting on it. The men in his army didn't have the same personal history with God, so they didn't have faith and doubted David had heard God's message correctly. God told David to go and fight and that he would win the battle, but God didn't give him the details. God expects us to obey His word and trust (have faith) that He will show us *what* to do and *when* to do it *after* we have taken the first step of obedience.

> *Faith isn't necessary if you know all the details.*

What was the result of the battle? (1 Samuel 23:5)

What thanks did David and his army get from the people of Keilah? (1 Samuel 23:7–12)

1 Samuel 23:13 is interesting. It says that David and his men went wherever they could go. It sounds like when they heard Saul coming, they scattered and hid wherever they could find room. Six hundred men, and their families would take up quite a bit of space and be hard to hide in one big group. David himself stayed in the strongholds located in the hill country of *Ziph*. There are many canyons and caves in this area of the desert that could hide small pockets of people.[1] Read Psalm 63, which David wrote while living in the deserts of Judah. What stands out to you about David's attitude from this Psalm?

Read 1 Samuel 23:14–29. According to these verses, Saul was hunting David every day. How stressful is that? We're told that Jonathan went to visit David at *Horesh* (a city near Ziph) to encourage him in God, and they restated their covenant of friendship. While David was at Horesh, the people of Ziph went to Saul and gave him specific locations to trap David. 1 Samuel 23:26 sets a tense scene that could have come straight from a movie set. David and his men are running on one side of the mountain, and Saul and his army are running on the other side trying to catch up. What would have happened if one of them had stopped or, better yet, run back the other way?

> *When you are surrounded, God will send His messenger to save you.*

Many Psalms of David were written while he was on the run from Saul. Read Psalm 18 and write down what David was feeling at the time and how he encouraged himself to keep going.

After intense battles, God will often bring times of refreshment. David next traveled about ten miles to Engedi where there was an oasis with natural springs. It was located southeast of Hebron above the shores of the Dead Sea and was known for its vineyards (Song of Solomon 1:14).[2] Of course, as soon as Saul heard where David was, he was back on the trail to hunt David down.

Read 1 Samuel 24:1–22. I'm sure David was getting tired of the chase, and so when Saul walked right into the cave where he was hiding, he could have thought God was delivering Saul into his hand, finally ending the long game of *hide-and-seek* they were play-ing. David's men urged him to do something to Saul and even made it sound like it was God's plan to harm Saul. But David still respected Saul as his father-in-law and his position as God's anointed king of Israel. What action did David take, and how did it make him feel after he did it?

Many times, we act out of frustration and say or do things that we later regret. Read Psalms 57 and 142. David wrote these words when he was in caves hiding from Saul. In several of the verses, he complains that there is no escape for him, and no one is concerned about his soul. It is so easy to become infected by other people's opin-ions. Both Saul and David made wrong choices based upon the input of the people closest to them.

If you start feeling stressed or angry while listening to someone else, you need to stop and consider why. Is it your emotion, or is it Satan infecting you with someone else's negative thoughts and emo-tions? We are told in Proverbs 4:23–24 to guard ourselves against evil input from others, and in Romans 12:18–21, Paul tells us that we are to *choose* peace, and we will overcome evil with good.

> *Choose your friends wisely—they will affect
> your choices for good or evil.*

1 Samuel 24:5 says that it was David's conscience that both-ered him for what might seem to be a small act of vandalism. Have you ever done something *small* that the Holy Spirit convicted you of, which you had to confess and make right with the other person involved? What happened when you confessed and tried to make it right?

> *Remember that it is up to the other person to accept or reject your apology. You are only responsible to offer it sincerely.*

Write out what 1 John 1:9 promises will happen if/when we confess our sins.

What does God promise to do in Isaiah 43:25?

How did Saul respond to David's confession and his vow not to harm Saul? (1 Samuel 24:16–22)

> *If God doesn't remember your sin—neither should you.*

In 1 Samuel 25:1, we read that Samuel has died, and all of Israel gathered to mourn him (usually a period of one week to one month). Isn't it just like God to time Samuel's death in the middle of a *cease-fire* so both David and Saul could pay their respects to his family? Afterward, David leaves and goes south to the *wilderness of Paran* near the city of *Maon*. This is the same area where the Israelites wandered and where Moses sent the twelve spies to check out the Promised Land. (See Numbers 10:12, 13:3–26.) We will cover what happened to David in the wilderness in our next chapter of study.

David then went back to the *hill country near Ziph.* The Ziphite people must have really wanted Saul to like them because they once again revealed to Saul that David was hiding near the hill of Hachilah. Read 1 Samuel 26:1–25 and keep in mind that Abishai (along with Joab) is David's nephew (his older sister is their mother Zeruiah). Because David had so many older siblings, these nephews may well have been close to him in age. Also remember that Abner was not only the commander of Saul's army but also his cousin. It was definitely a family affair. This is the last recorded encounter between David and Saul. What bad advice did Abishai give to David, and what was David's response? (1 Samuel 26:8–10)

What did David do instead—what did he take from Saul? (1 Samuel 26:11–12)

What does 1 Samuel 26:12 say about the sleep of Saul's army? Could David's action be God's idea?

David's conscience didn't bother him this time. How was this act different than cutting off Saul's robe?

What was David's logical argument to Saul in 1 Samuel 26:17–20 and 22–24?

In 1 Samuel 24:14, David went from calling himself a dead dog and a single flea to just the single flea in 1 Samuel 26:20. Why do you think David used this image to describe his relationship to Saul?

What was Saul's response? (1 Samuel 26:21–25)

Psalm 54 was written during this time period. Write down what David says about the people of Ziph and what he says about God.
People of Ziph:

God:

Satan will use other people to draw you back into a fight that you already won. He enjoys stirring up strife in relationships that have already made peace.

Beware who you are listening to even if they are friends and family. You *must* listen to the Spirit of peace and wisdom. Always consider the source of the opinion! Write out Proverbs 22:24–25 below and memorize it this week.

Read 1 Samuel 27:1–7. As we have already seen in 1 Samuel 21:10, it seems crazy that David would go back to the Philistine king Achish for protection, but as we read here, his plan worked. Saul stopped chasing him. What does 1 Samuel 27:1 say about David's thoughts/reasoning?

How long did David and his men live in the Philistine territories? (1 Samuel 27:7)

David was a long way from the simple life of his childhood. He was no longer a simple shepherd boy protecting his father's sheep. He was now a shepherd of men, women, and children, all while being considered a traitor by his own people. Read what David had to say to encourage himself in Psalm 23 and Psalm 138.

Which verses mean the most to you and why?

As I mentioned before, I am writing this study guide in 2020, the year of COVID-19. I am also providing personal and logistical support for my aging parents. So between writing a book, helping my parents, and wearing a mask everywhere I go, I encourage myself by speaking Psalm 138:8 over myself every morning. I recommend that you look it up, write it down, and put it somewhere you can see every morning. Speak it out loud over yourself each day and be encouraged.

Read 1 Samuel 27:5–28:2 to understand what David and his men were doing during the sixteen months they lived within Philistia. Why did king Achish give David the city of Ziklag? (1 Samuel 27:5–6)

Would you have been bold enough to ask a foreign king for a city of your own? What does that say about David's confidence level?

Read 1 Chronicles 12:1–22. Who were the men who joined David's army while he was in Ziklag?

How are these warriors described?

David's army had grown from the original three hundred men to four hundred men to now being described as a great army, like the army of God. Many men from the other eleven tribes of Israel were defecting from Saul's army to join David's army.

Find Ziklag on the map in the back of your Bible. It is about twenty miles south of Gath, so David probably felt very safe to raid cities that were south of Ziklag. He didn't raid any cities to the north that were between his city and Gath.

Why did David kill everything and everyone in the cities he raided? (1 Samuel 27:9, 11)

Do you think that it was okay for David to tell a "white" lie to King Achish about his activities? Why or why not? (1 Samuel 27:10, 12)

We have seen David lie several times in the book of First Samuel, and yet he was called a man after God's own heart (1 Samuel 13:14; Acts 13:22). In Genesis, Abraham lied several times to save himself, and yet he too was highly favored by God. (See Genesis 12:11–20 and all of Genesis 20.) Jesus said that any time a person tells a lie, they are being most like Satan. (See John 8:44.)

How does this apply to your life today? Believers in Jesus Christ have been saved from their sins through grace, but in the sixth chapter of Romans, Paul tells us that we must not continue to live in sin. God knows that we will mess up on a daily basis if we don't listen to the Holy Spirit who is willing to help us make the right choices. Remember that Samuel asked God what to say to Saul so that he wouldn't have to tell a lie (1 Samuel 16:2–5). We have the power within us to make the right choice, and if we ask for wisdom, God has promised to give it to us freely (James 1:5).

What honor did king Achish bestow on David that showed his high level of trust and respect? (1 Samuel 28:1–2)

Do you think God made sure that Achish gave David such favor to keep him protected from the rest of the Philistine lords who didn't like (or trust) David?

What do these Scriptures tell you about God's favor?
Psalm 5:12

Psalm 84:11–12

Psalm 90:17

Proverbs 3:1–4

Proverbs 8:35–36

Bonus study: Bible people God gave favor

Esther, 2:8–9, 15–18, and 5:2; Joseph, Genesis 39:2–4, 21, and 41:38–44; Daniel, Daniel 1:9 and 19–21; Moses, Exodus 33:17; Mary, Luke 1:30; Ruth, 2:10–13; Samuel, 1 Samuel 2:26

Read 1 Samuel 29. Do you think that God protected David from participating in the battle against Israel by causing the Philistine lords to tell King Achish that David couldn't come with them?

Have you ever started to do something you knew was wrong, and God intervened and stopped you? What was your reaction?

King Achish never found anything wrong in David (1 Samuel 29:6) because God protected David from Achish discovering all the raids he had done against the neighboring cities. God protected David, not because he was perfect and did everything right but because God is good, and He protects His children.

Read Psalm 91:14–16 and Psalm 145:20. Are you a child of God? If you have asked Jesus to be your Lord and Savior, then these verses are true for you today. If you don't have a personal relationship with Jesus, you can start right now! Go to the back of this study guide for information to help you begin your new life with Jesus Christ.

The Wives of David

Michal

In 1 Samuel 18:20–28, we learn the circumstances of David's first marriage to Saul's youngest daughter, Michal. It says that she loved David and proved it by protecting David's life when her father sent men to kill him (1 Samuel 19:11–17). When David went on the run, Michal stayed behind in her father's house. When Saul became frustrated with David and understood he was not coming back, Saul gave Michal to become another man's wife (1 Samuel 25:44). You can read more about Michal's reunion with David in 2 Samuel 3:14–16 and 2 Samuel 6:16–23. From these Scriptures, we can assume that her feelings of love turned into bitterness and hate just as her father's *love* turned to murderous hatred of David.

It's hard not to feel somewhat sorry for Michal as she was used as a pawn in men's hands: first her father and then David. She was separated from David through no fault of her own (unless David offered for her to go on the run with him and she said no), and then her father gave her to another man in marriage. (Was it even legal since David was still alive?) Then when David became king, he asked to get her back (possibly to reaffirm his legal connection to the house of Saul), and though we aren't told how Michal felt about it, we are told how deeply her new husband grieved (2 Samuel 3:16).

We can assume that Michal wasn't happy to learn that David now had six other wives (2 Samuel 3:1–4). The last thing we hear about Michal (after she made negative comments about David) is that she was barren and never had children. This might be because David never again treated her as his wife, or it is quite possible that she was already barren because she didn't have any children with her second husband either. Michal's life became totally barren; everyone she had loved had been taken from her. There were so many broken dreams, after what had seemed like a fairy tale beginning to her life.

Can you relate to Michal? Did you start out in a *dream situation* but end up in a lonely place with no joy and only the bitterness of an unfulfilled dream in your heart? Allow God to meet you in your lonely place; *let* His love fill you and *choose* to believe that He is good.

> This is a choice that must be made each and every time Satan offers you feelings of self-pity, bitterness, or insecurity. Choose to believe that God is good and He can make all things work together for your good. (Romans 8:28)

What is God's answer to loneliness and betrayal?
Psalm 25:16–18

Psalm 27:9–10

Psalm 68:5–6

Isaiah 41:9–10

Romans 8:31–39

Abigail

Read 1 Samuel 25. This is the story of Nabal, his wife Abigail, and how their lives intersected with David and his men. How is Nabal described? (1 Samuel 25:2–3, 17, 25)

What do these verses say about Abigail? (1 Samuel 25:3, 17–19, 24–25, 28, 32–33, 36–37, 39–42)

Why was David in the vicinity of Maon (wilderness of Paran)? (1 Samuel 23:24–28)

Why did David send the ten young men to speak to Nabal? (1 Samuel 25:5–8)

What was David's reasoning behind the request? (1 Samuel 25:21)

Because Nabal had so many sheep, he sent his shepherds south to the wilderness of Paran where they could forage on the mountain grasses. Big ranches still do this today (Montana and many more), sending their livestock up to graze in the mountain meadows allowing their own field a rest from grazing. In the late fall, the animals are gathered and brought back down to the ranch. The animals have gained weight on the good grazing ground at no cost to the rancher. They are healthy and have gained weight, which will bring in better prices when sold. It is a win/win situation for the rancher. One drawback is that in the wilderness, the animals are open to any predators living on the mountain. This is why David said that he and his men had protected Nabal's animals from any harm.

How did Nabal respond to David's request? (1 Samuel 25:10–11)

Do you think David had a *right* to ask Nabal for supplies if they didn't have a prior agreement? Why or why not?

David *chose* to be offended and got angry because his *expectation* was not met. Nabal didn't respond the way David had imagined. So many times, we tell ourselves *stories* of how things will happen, and then *real life* happens.

Have you ever chosen to be offended when someone didn't react the way you expected?

What does God say about choosing to become offended?
Proverbs 18:19

Proverbs 19:11

Romans 12:17–21

2 Timothy 2:24

James 1:19–20

Who told Abigail what happened between Nabal and David's messengers? (1 Samuel 25:14–17)

List what Abigail gave to David and his men. (1 Samuel 25:18)

First Samuel 25:18 tells us that the food supplies were already prepared. What was the food supposed to be used for? (1 Samuel 25:11)

What does it say about Abigail's character that she didn't just send the supplies with the servants but got on a donkey and went herself to meet David? (1 Samuel 25:20, 23)

In 1 Samuel 25:29, Abigail revealed that she knew the story of David killing Goliath because she used the example of his enemies being thrown by God's slingshot. What did Abigail say that showed she also understood the spiritual side of David's problem with Nabal and the bigger call of God on his life? (1 Samuel 25:26–31)

How did David respond to Abigail's speech? (1 Samuel 25:32–35)

In 1 Samuel 25:28, Abigail protects her servants' lives by taking the blame for Nabal's negative answer to David's request for supplies. Then in 1 Samuel 25:36–37, we see her wisdom to choose the right time (as well as her courage) to speak the truth of her actions to Nabal even if it might cost her personal safety (if he got angry with her). What happened to Nabal when Abigail told him what she had done? (1 Samuel 25:36–38)

Who does it say struck Nabal down? (1 Samuel 25:38)

This passage says that Nabal's heart died within him and it became as a stone, but he didn't die until ten days later. It sounds like a good description of a heart attack and/or stroke, possibly the physical outcome of a fit of anger?

What was David's response to the news? (1 Samuel 25:39–40)

Read 1 Samuel 25:40–43. I noticed that the messenger came to Abigail at Carmel, not in Maon where Nabal's house was located. This might mean that she had been removed from her home because she had no son to inherit the property, and it went to one of Nabal's relatives. If this was the case, then it gave Abigail even more reason to accept David's offer of marriage. The female servants mentioned may have been the only personal resources she had; perhaps they had accompanied her from her father's house upon her marriage. These women may have been her only emotional support while living with a terrible husband, and she rewarded their loyalty by bringing them with her to join David's household. We aren't told how she responded to moving to a foreign country or living with the other woman who David took as his wife while he was on the run.

How would you have felt if you were Abigail? Relieved? Scared? Excited? Or would you have taken offense that David didn't come to offer you marriage in person?

Ahinoam of Jezreel (1 Samuel 27:3)

We aren't told anything more about Ahinoam except in 1 Chronicles 3:1 where it says she bore David his first son, Amnon. An article by Linda Schering in "The Encyclopedia of Jewish Women" comments that there is only one other person named Ahinoam in the Bible and that is the wife of King Saul in 1 Samuel 14:50. Therefore, it suggested it is possible that Ahinoam of Jezreel is the same woman as Saul's wife. Second Samuel 12:8 is used as evidence of this. Nathan, the prophet of God, tells David that God had given him his master's house and his master's wives into his care. It is implied that David's marriage to Saul's wife would solidify his right to become the next king of Israel.[1]

I personally believe that they are two separate women. The timeline of David's marriage to Ahinoam of Jezreel occurs while Saul is still alive, so it does not make sense that Saul's wife Ahinoam would leave him and go on the run with David. She was also much older than David and had already borne five children, including David's friend Jonathan (1 Samuel 14:49–50). I think the reason that it always refers to her as Ahinoam of Jezreel proves the need to differentiate David's wife from Saul's wife who is noted as Ahinoam the daughter of Ahimaaz. The comment from Nathan could mean that besides David's care of Jonathan's son Mephibosheth (2 Samuel 9), David could have also put Saul's widow into the care of his other wives and concubines out of respect for her as Jonathan's mother.

THE WIVES OF DAVID

David married three women (Michal, Ahinoam, Abigail) before he became Judah's king at the age of thirty. During the next seven-and-one-half years in Hebron, he married four more women (Maacah, Haggith, Abital, and Eglah) and had a child by six of these women (2 Samuel 3:2–5). He then married Bathsheba after becoming king over all Israel and moving to set up his kingdom in Jerusalem. (See 2 Samuel 11.)

We know from 1 Chronicles 3:1–9 that David married eight women, and 2 Samuel 15:16 tells us he also had at least ten concubines (unnamed). Six sons were born to David while he was in Hebron as king over Judah and then thirteen more boys and a girl named Tamar were born in Jerusalem when he was king over all Israel. This passage also tells us that there were other unnamed daughters and sons of David's concubines but doesn't tell us how many children in total.

Saul Fails the Leadership Test

We skipped over 1 Samuel 28 while we were following David on the run. Read 1 Samuel 28:3–25 and answer the following questions. Why had Saul removed all the mediums and spiritists (people who speak to the dead) from the land? (See Deuteronomy 18: 9–15.)

Who was Saul supposed to ask for wisdom and help to make decisions?

It's interesting that Saul tried to get an answer from the Lord (1 Samuel 28:6), but the Lord didn't answer him. According to Psalm 66:18 and Proverbs 1:7, why didn't God respond to his prayer?

Have you ever prayed with the wrong heart attitude and not received an answer? Read Hebrews 11:6, James 1:5–8, and 1 Peter 3:7–12. What are the prerequisites to getting your prayers heard and answered?

> *If God has already told you to do something and you haven't obeyed, don't expect to hear anything new. It didn't work for Jonah and it won't work for you. (Jonah 1:1–3, 3:1–3)*

Saul had proven to no longer fear God himself; he was going through the motions, but his heart was not connected to God's heart. When Saul didn't get an answer from God, he chose to seek direction through an ungodly, demonic source: a medium. I believe that Saul really wanted to ask the prophet Samuel for help, and this was the only way he could think of doing it (1 Samuel 28:15). The medium lived in Endor, which was located in the far north, five to ten miles north of Mount Gilboa (where the Israeli army would fight the Philistines the next day).

Who told Saul how to find the medium? (1 Samuel 28:7)

What was the punishment for anyone acting as a medium? (Leviticus 20:27)

When I was a child, Ouija boards were in every toy store board game section, and everyone knew their astrological birth sign. The question "what's your sign?" even became a clichéd pick-up line in the 1970s. Have you ever sought wisdom/direction for your life from a demonic source, horoscopes, palm readers, Ouija boards, tarot cards, and the like? Today, there are many people who make their living by speaking to the dead, and many television shows and movies portray a medium as their main character. Satan will always answer those who seek him for guidance with words that speak to the lust of their eyes, the lust of their flesh, and their pride in life. Satan is *always* a liar! (John 8:44)

What do these Scriptures say about it? (Genesis 3:4–6; James 1:13–15; 1 John 2:15–18)

When you open the door to Satan, you will get much more than you asked for. If you have opened a door in your life in any of these ways, take the time right now to confess it to Jesus and turn away from ever opening yourself to it again. Renounce any unholy agreements that you made in the past and claim the blood of Jesus to wash away any stain of it from your life. Ask the Holy Spirit to fill you up and cleanse all those areas where you allowed demonic influences to rule your life.

What did Saul do before leaving his house to travel to Endor? (1 Samuel 28:8)

Saul didn't want the Israelite army to know that he was leaving camp. He disguised himself (probably wearing the clothes of a servant) and snuck out into the darkness. One thing he could not hide was his height. He did take a couple of bodyguards with him because the enemy camp was close by.

We aren't told if the medium was a gentile or a Hebrew woman, but it was clear she knew the law said she would get the death penalty if she was caught in the act. Saul had to reassure her that he wouldn't turn her in if/when he didn't like the result of his visit (It was always a risk she took when giving someone bad news.)

What did Saul vow/swear by to prove he was telling the truth? (1 Samuel 28:10)

Do you think that this could be considered taking the Lord's name in vain (wrongful use/blasphemy) since Saul had already proven he had no fear or respect for God?

What does Exodus 20:7 say will happen to someone who uses the name of God inappropriately?

Do you ever swear to prove your statements are true? What did Jesus say about swearing in Matthew 5:33–37?

It is evident that the medium did not know who Samuel was by name and did not recognize Saul. What happened when she saw Samuel? (1 Samuel 28:11–12)

How did she describe Samuel? (1 Samuel 28:13–14)

> *In heaven, we have new bodies but we will still be*
> *able to recognize each other. See 1 Corinthians 13:12,*
> *Philippians 3:20–21, and Matthew 17:2–4.*

When the medium called Samuel, he came up from "Abraham's bosom" and wanted to know why his rest was being disturbed. In the Old Testament, when God's people died, their spirits went to a place called "Abraham's bosom," which was located in Sheol. It was a place of waiting and rest. (See Luke 16:19–31, Jonah 2:2, and Psalm 16:10.) Since Jesus had not yet died for their sins, these followers of God were held *captive* in this place. On the cross, Jesus said that he and the thief would be in "Paradise" together that same day (See Luke 23:43).

After three days in this place, Jesus rose from the dead, and Daniel 7:13–14 tells us that Jesus led these captives (cloud of witnesses) to the throne room of God where Jesus presented Himself as the blood sacrifice for the sins of the whole world, and God gave Him everlasting dominion. (See also John 20:17, Psalm 68:18, Ephesians 4:7–10, Hebrews 12:1–2, and Revelation 2:7.) Today when a follower of Jesus dies, they do not have to wait. They are immediately with Jesus in heaven (2 Corinthians 5:6–8) where they join the cloud of witnesses around the throne of God.

What was Samuel's reaction to Saul's summons? (1 Samuel 28:15)

What reason did Samuel give for God not answering Saul's prayer? (1 Samuel 28:16–18)

What news did Saul receive from Samuel that caused him to faint in fear? (1 Samuel 28:19–21)

Even though the medium did not fear God, she still feared the power of Saul. When she saw Saul's reaction to Samuel's bad news, what did she do to show her compassion and concern for Saul's well-being? (1 Samuel 28:21–25)

The medium may have wanted to give Saul something to eat to strengthen him for his journey. But the other possibility is that she gave Saul food to ensure that he was able to leave quickly. The longer he stayed, the more time he had for second thoughts.

Remember that Saul had taken this trip in secret with two other men. We aren't told if they heard what Samuel had said would happen in the battle or not. If they didn't hear, would you have told them or kept it to yourself? Would you still have gone into battle the next day, knowing that you and your sons would die in it?

Read the end result of the battle in 1 Samuel 31. Who was killed besides Saul?

Saul's youngest son, Ish-bosheth (in his late thirties), was not in this war, or if he was, he was not killed in it. After the death of Saul and three of his sons, Abner, Saul's cousin and commander of the army, took over the rule of Israel in a type of military dictatorship for five years. Then when the elders of Israel began asking for a king, Abner took Ish-bosheth and put him on the throne of Israel. He led the eleven tribes of Israel into a civil war with the followers of David and the tribe of Judah for seven years. I cover this time of Israel's history in my next study guide on the book of Second Samuel titled *The Life of David: A Series of Unfortunate Events*. You can read about it right now in 2 Samuel 2–3, and then Ish-bosheth's murder is described in 2 Samuel 4.

How does Saul die according to 1 Samuel 31:3–5?

Compare this to the rest of the story found in 2 Samuel 1:1–10. How did Saul really die?

What did the Philistines do with the bodies of Saul and his sons? (1 Samuel 31:8–10)

This seems gruesome to us now, but at that time in world history, it was how a nation publicized news of their victory in war. Remember that David cut off Goliath's head and carried it to Jerusalem to be buried. All along the way, people would have seen Goliath's decapitated head and understood Israel's victory over the Philistines. Today, we see the results of war in graphic pictures of the dead bodies of soldiers as well as innocent women and children on the daily news reports. Little really has changed in three thousand years.

Remember the men of Jabesh-Gilead that Saul saved in his very first battle as king of Israel? (1 Samuel 11) How did they honor Saul's memory? (1 Samuel 31:11–13)

What was the personal cost these men paid to retrieve the bodies of Saul and his sons?

Just as Saul and his army had marched all through the night to arrive in time to save Jabesh-Gilead from the Ammonites, these same men walked all night to retrieve the body parts of Saul and his sons. Then they walked all the way back home to cremate and bury the bones and ashes. Since handling dead bodies made the men "unclean" (Numbers 19:11–13), they grieved and fasted for an entire week, fulfilling the law.

Have you ever shown loyalty to someone even when it cost you? Would you have been counted among these men?

How are we to show our loyalty to the one who saved us from death (eternal)?

John 3:16–21

2 Corinthians 5:14–21

How did David reward the men of Jabesh-Gilead in 2 Samuel 2:4–6?

Are you willing to follow Jesus even if/when it costs you something: money, popularity, time, and energy? Stop and speak a vow of loyalty to Jesus right now.

David Passes the Leadership Test

The last chapters of First Samuel reveal final scenes full of high drama. While Saul has been out visiting the medium of Endor, David and his men have become a source of conflict between king Achish and the other five Philistine lords. Read 1 Samuel 29. After a three-day trip, David and his men return to their home city of Ziklag to find that the Amalekites had attacked while they were gone.

Many times in life, the greatest tests follow a great victory. Satan likes to attack when we are tired and perhaps feeling a little pride in our achievements. Read 1 Samuel 30 and answer the following questions:

What did the Amalekites do to the city of Ziklag?

What did the Amalekites take away with them?

What was the miracle in 1 Samuel 30:2?

How did David's men react?

We are told that even though both of David's wives, Abigail and Ahinoam, were taken captive, David's main heartache was caused by his men. What did the men want to do to David?

Bonus study on stoning as a form of capital punishment

Numbers 15:35–36; Deuteronomy 21:18–21; Leviticus 20:2 and 24:16; John 8:4–11 and 10:31–33; and Acts 7:54–60

It seems to be human nature that when things go wrong in our lives, we want to blame the people in authority for our problems. Each of these men had chosen of their own free will to follow David. They had seen God protect David and save their lives over and over during the past eight years while running away from Saul, and yet when a terrible event occurred to all of them (David included), they showed no loyalty to David and spoke of stoning him. Logically speaking, stoning David would not have brought their families back.

This was another attempt by Satan to kill God's anointed king and the generational lineage of Jesus Christ, the future Savior of mankind who would defeat Satan once for all at the cross. What does 1 Samuel 30:6 say was David's response to the men's threats?

Turn *to* God not *against* others

How did David encourage himself? Read Psalm 3:3 and 5:1–3. Both of these Psalms have been sung as worship songs. If you know them, stop and sing the words right out of your Bible in praise and worship to God just like David did.

Here are some steps that David took to encourage himself in God from Psalm 18:1–3 and 18, Psalm 42:5 and 11, and Psalm 43:5 that you can apply to your own life today.

Go to God with your pain—pour out your feelings.

Remember God's goodness and faithfulness in the past.

Receive His peace and healing for your emotions.

Ask God what to do next (if anything).

Receive and believe the words that God gives you.

Step out in faith.

What did David do to find out God's will? (1 Samuel 30:7–8)

The description of an ephod is found in Exodus 28:6–35. It was a robe worn by the high priest into the Holy of Holies where God's presence remained above the mercy seat on top of the Ark of the Covenant. The breastplate was a pouch worn over the ephod, and it contained the "Urim and Thummim" used to cast lots. The breastplate was covered with twelve precious stones, each engraved with a name of Jacob's twelve sons (Israel's tribes). When the high priest wore the ephod into the Holy of Holies, he was representing the entire nation of Israel to God. Read Hebrews 4:14–16 and 7:25–27. Who is the believer's high priest today?

How does knowing Jesus as your high priest affect your life today? (John 14:12–14)

What was the good news God told David? (1 Samuel 30:8)

How do you know that David believed what God said?

Faith without action is not really faith (James 2:18). God said that *all* would be rescued. *But it became true only after David gathered his men and went after the Amalekites.* Using your own words, write out Hebrews 11:1, adding what situations you are in right now.

For example, I could say—"Faith is the assurance that since God told me to write this study guide, I can believe that He will give me a publisher that accepts it, and I am convinced that He will provide the money to pay for it."

What do you say? Faith is…

How did David *show* that the Spirit of God was giving him wisdom in his treatment of the Egyptian slave they found? (1 Samuel 30:11–16)

DAVID PASSES THE LEADERSHIP TEST

Compare David's actions to the following Scriptures:
Proverbs 25:21–22

Romans 12:19–21

Matthew 25:34–46

How did God bless David for his treatment of the Egyptian slave? (1 Samuel 30:18–19)

Have you ever experienced God's blessing in your life after you had helped someone else? We shouldn't serve others with selfish motives, believing that if we do something good by helping others, God now *owes* us something. As we read in Matthew 25, God looks at the intents of our heart (why we do it) and judges us accordingly. Why/how should we serve others then?

Numbers 1:45 tells us that the Israeli army is made up of men from the age of twenty and upward. There is no ending (retirement) age given. In Joshua 14:7–12, we read that Caleb was forty years old when he was sent to spy out the Promised Land, and after forty years in the wilderness, he was still a leader in the fighting when Israel finally entered the land. At the age of eighty-five, Caleb was still full of energy and strength. We also know that Saul died in battle at the age of seventy-two (1 Samuel 13:1, 31:1–6).

The two hundred men in David's army who stayed behind with the baggage at the brook (1 Samuel 30:10) may well have been in their sixties and seventies. If you think of the situation that way, it makes sense that David stood up for them and gave these older men a share equal to the younger warriors who went into the battle. It's also important to notice that this was not the first time two hundred men were left behind with the baggage while the other men went off to fight. (See 1 Samuel 25:13.)

What did the wicked and worthless men among David's army say about the two hundred men who had stayed behind at the brook with the supplies/baggage this time? (1 Samuel 30:21–22)

What was David's response to these men and how did it affect the future actions of Israel's army? (1 Samuel 30:23–25)

It's interesting to read that out of the six hundred men who joined David's army and fought together for over eight years, there were still some who were wicked and enjoyed stirring up strife among the others. You can still see this same effect today in offices, governments, churches, and families. Anywhere you have a group of people gathering together, there will be those who are not walking with God, and Satan uses their minds, mouths, and actions to stir up anger and strife within the group.

How can you apply these Scriptures to your life today?
Proverbs 10:11–12

Proverbs 16:28–29

Proverbs 28:25–28

Proverbs 29:22

James 3:6–18

Matthew 7:13–23

Satan Works through People, but so Does God

What did David do with his share of the spoils to show his thankfulness to all his supporters? (1 Samuel 30:26–31)

David understood the importance of giving back to those who had been there when he needed help. He recognized that everyone who helped him was considered a traitor by Saul, and by helping David, they risked their own lives, as well as the lives of their families. Notice that there are over fourteen different cities/territories in this list of people who supported David during his eight years on the run from Saul.

It was these same elders of Judah who first placed David on the throne. He chose to rule from Hebron for the first seven-and-one-half years of his reign. (See 2 Samuel 2:1–4 and 5:1–7)

Life Lesson from David's Battle Plan: Leave the Baggage Behind

You cannot fight the enemy if you are holding on/carrying your old baggage. The baggage could be from childhood experiences, past relationships, broken dreams, or unfulfilled expectations. Jesus said that He came to set us free by telling us truth. Face up to the truth of the past and then let it go. As long as you choose to hang on to past hurts and offenses, Satan's lies will win the battle, and you will remain in bondage. Be like David; leave the baggage with others in the past, and you will be free to enjoy the victory found in the good future Jesus died to give you!

Last Thought about First Samuel

Samuel was the only person to hold the position of judge, prophet, and priest at the same time.

David was the only person to hold the position of judge, prophet, and king at the same time.

Jesus is the only One who fulfills all of these positions: Prophet, Priest, Judge, and King.

- Jesus as Prophet: Matthew 21:11; Luke 7:16; and John 4:19
- Jesus as Priest: Hebrews 2:17–18, 4:14–16, and 5:5–10
- Jesus as Judge: Acts 10:42–43, 17:30–31; and 2 Corinthians 5:10
- Jesus as King: Isaiah 9:6–7; John 18:36–37; and Revelation 19:11–16

Conclusion

There are so many interesting people and dramatic events in this first book of Samuel that it is difficult to pick a favorite story line. Each person had strengths as well as weaknesses, which proves that these were real people. God made sure that we saw the good and the bad things that happened in their lives, allowing us the time and space to learn from, and hopefully, not repeat their mistakes in our own lives.

Our quality of life depends upon our willingness to listen to God and obey what we hear. I hope and pray that you heard God's voice speaking into your life through His Word and that you enjoyed the study of First Samuel.

Now that you have completed your study of First Samuel, I encourage you to study other books of the Old Testament. I have written a study guide on the minor prophets of the Old Testament called *12 Ordinary Men Who Lived Extraordinary Lives: A Study Guide on the Minor Prophets* that you might enjoy. It is published by Christian Faith Publishing and is available on Amazon. I am currently writing a study guide on the book of Second Samuel for publishing as well.

The Word of God is still alive and active, and God will use *all* of His Word to transform your life—if you let it.

Until next time we study together.

Blessings,
Diane

How to Begin a Relationship with Jesus

If you have not yet asked Jesus to come into your life, here is what you need to know.

The Bible says that we are all sinful people because the very first man (Adam) sinned. Everyone born after Adam inherits the genetic condition to sin, and we all do and say bad things. Jesus never sinned, and because He was perfect when He died on the cross, He took all of our sins (past/present/future) onto Himself, and God accepted His punishment in our place. The Bible also says that if we agree that we have sinned and believe that Jesus died in our place, we can ask Jesus to come and live within us. He promises that He will and that when we die, we will go to heaven to live with Him.

> Jesus saith unto him, I am the way, the truth, and the life: no man cometh unto the Father, but by me. (John 14:6 KJV)

> For God so loved the world that he gave his only begotten Son, that whosoever believeth in Him should not perish, but have everlasting life. For God sent not his Son into the world to condemn the world; but that the world through him might be saved. (John 3:16–17 KJV)

> But God commendeth his love toward us, in that, while we were yet sinners, Christ died for us much more then, being now justified by his blood, we shall be saved from wrath through him. For if, when we were enemies, we were rec-

onciled to God by the death of his Son, much more, being reconciled, we shall be saved by his life. And not only so, but we also joy in God through our Lord Jesus Christ, by whom we have now received the atonement. (Romans 5:8–11 KJV)

That if thou shalt confess with thy mouth the Lord Jesus, and shalt believe in thine heart that God hath raised him from the dead, thou shalt be saved. For with the heart man believeth unto righteousness; and with the mouth confession is made unto salvation. (Romans 10:9–10 KJV)

And this is the record that God hath given to us eternal life, and this life is in his Son. He that hath the Son hath life; and he that hath not the Son of God hath not life. These things have I written unto you that believe on the name of the Son of God; that ye may know that ye have eternal life, and that ye may believe on the name of the Son of God. (1 John 5:11–13 KJV)

To begin a relationship with Jesus, pray this prayer (or one like it) *out loud*: "Dear Jesus, I believe that you are the Son of God. I believe that You died on the cross for my sins and that because You rose from the dead. When I die, I will also rise from the dead to be with You in heaven. Please come into my heart and take away all my sins: past, present, and future, and baptize me in the Holy Spirit (See Acts 2:1–18 and 10:38–48).

Thank you that Holy Spirit is now living in me and confirms to me that I am God's child. Amen. (See Romans 8:14–16.)

Notes

Background of the Book of First Samuel

[1] *Wikipedia*, "Books of Samuel," accessed on 12/26/2020.
[2] *Wikipedia*, "Samuel (name)," accessed on 12/2/2020.

Family Drama

[1] Biu.ac.il, Bar-Ilan University's Parashat Hashavua Study Center Parashat Toledot 5766/December 4, 2005, "For she was barren": Infertility as grounds for divorce," Dr. Yoel Shiloh, Ashkelon College, accessed on 12/3/2020.

Loss of the Ark

[1] *Ryrie Study Bible,* New American Standard, Charles Caldwell Ryrie, Th.D., Ph.D., Moody Bible Institute of Chicago, 1978, p. 419.
[2] Scripture taken from the *Tree of Life Version,* Copyright 2015 by the Messianic Jewish Family Bible Society. Used by permission of the Messianic Jewish Family Bible Society.

Samuel's Ministry Begins

[1] *Halley's Bible Handbook*, New Revised Edition, Henry H. Halley, Zondervan Publishing, 1965, p. 166.
[2] *Britannica*, "Ancient deity, Baal," accessed on 12/4/2020.
[3] *Wikipedia*, "Charging bull, Wall Street Bull," accessed on 12/4/2020.
[4] Joyce Meyer, *Knowing God Intimately*, https://quotefamncy.com, "sitting in a garage won't make you a car."

The Making of a King: Saul

[1] Scripture taken from the *Tree of Life Version*, Copyright 2015, by the Messianic Jewish Family Bible Society. Used by permission of the Messianic Jewish Family Bible Society.

NOTES

Blueletterbible, Don Stewart, 469: "What is the Word of Knowledge?" accessed on 12/7/2020.

Saul's Early Years as King

[1] Ryrie Study Bible, New American Standard, Charles Caldwell Ryrie, Th.D., Ph.D., Moody Bible Institute of Chicago, 1978, p. 425.

David Enters the Scene

[1] TheJewishWoman.org, Nitzeret, Mother of David, Article by Chana Weisberg, "The bold voice of silence," accessed on 1/7/2021.
[2] *Ducksters*, history, Cyrus the Great, "Ancient Mesopotamia Biography of Cyrus the Great," accessed on 3/8/21.
[3] Independent.co.uk, News, Science, "Scientists prove it really is a thin line between love and hate", 10/29/20080.
[4] *Merriam-Webster*, cubit, span.
[5] Vocabulary.com, quarantine.
[6] "Golgotha: The Word Symbolizes Beautiful Reality!" by Dr. Taylor Marshall, taylormmarshall.com, accessed on 12/10/2020.

David's Life on the Run

[1] *Ryrie Study Bible*, New American Standard, Charles Caldwell Ryrie, Th.D., Ph.D., Moody Bible Institute of Chicago, 1978, p. 447.
[2] *Ryrie Study Bible*, New American Standard, Charles Caldwell Ryrie, Th.D., Ph.D., Moody Bible Institute of Chicago, 1978, p. 448.

The Wives of David

[1] jwa.org, "The Encyclopedia of Jewish Women," Ahinoam: Bible, article by Linda Schearing, accessed on 12/16/2020.

About the Author

Diane Rafferty made Jesus her Savior at the age of seven, but He became her Lord at the age of seventeen when she heard God speak to her directly from His Word.

Diane feels that her life purpose is to help people mature and grow in their love and knowledge of God's love letter—the Bible—and to encourage followers of Jesus to actively seek to hear God's voice and see His power released into their daily lives as they spend time in God's Word.

Diane has been married for over forty years (to the same man!) and lives in Washington state. She has two adult children and seven grandchildren.

CPSIA information can be obtained
at www.ICGtesting.com
Printed in the USA
JSHW022346280622
27452JS00002B/68